Who Should Own
Natural Resources?

T0056396

Political Theory Today series

Margaret Moore

———————

Who Should Own Natural Resources?

polity

First published in 2019 by Polity Press

Polity Press
65 Bridge Street
Cambridge CB2 1UR, UK

Polity Press
101 Station Landing
Suite 300
Medford, MA 02155, USA

ISBN-13: 978-1-5095-2916-2
ISBN-13: 978-1-5095-2917-9(pb)

A catalogue record for this book is available from the British Library.

Library of Congress Cataloging-in-Publication Data

Names: Moore, Margaret (Professor in Political Theory), author.
Title: Who should own natural resources? / Margaret Moore.
Description: Medford, MA : Polity, 2019. | Series: Political theory today | Includes bibliographical references and index.
Identifiers: LCCN 2018057111 (print) | LCCN 2019004998 (ebook) | ISBN 9781509529193 (Epub) | ISBN 9781509529162 (hardback) | ISBN 9781509529179 (pbk.)
Subjects: LCSH: Natural resources--Management. | Conservation of natural resources.
Classification: LCC HC85 (ebook) | LCC HC85 .M65 2019 (print) | DDC 333.01--dc23
LC record available at https://lccn.loc.gov/2018057111

Typeset in 11 on 15 Sabon by Servis Filmsetting Ltd, Stockport, Cheshire
Printed and bound in Great Britain by TJ International Ltd

For further information on Polity, visit our website: politybooks.com

Contents

Acknowledgements

I wrote this book while I was an Olof Palme Professor at Stockholm University in autumn, 2018. I am very appreciative of this opportunity and have a number of organizations and people to thank. I am grateful to the Swedish Research Council for funding this professorship; Stockholm University for nominating and hosting me; and Ludvig Beckman, Markus Furendaal and Michele Micheletti for help with the logistics and putting together the nomination. I am also grateful to the Social Sciences and Humanities Research Council of Canada for a research grant that funded part of this research. For comments on some parts of the arguments, given at the Australian National University; Universidad Panamericano; the Institute for Future Studies, Stockholm; University of Pavia; Uppsala University; and University of Bayreuth, I am grateful to Arash

Acknowledgements

Abizadeh, Gustaf Arrhenius, Ludvig Beckman, Ian Carter, Eva Erman, Luis Xavier López Farjeat, Bob Goodin, Gina Gustavsson, Andrew Lister, Sofia Näsström, Alice Pinhciro-Walla, Hans Roth, Nic Southwood and Christine Straehle, as well as audiences at these venues. I am especially grateful to Patti Lenard, David Miller and the two anonymous readers for Polity Press for extremely helpful and insightful comments on the complete first draft, and to George Owers and Julia Davies of Polity Press, who were both encouraging and critical at different times, which helped me to transform this into a better short book than it would otherwise have been.

1

Introduction

This book advances a theory of justice in natural resources. There are more than seven billion people on Earth, a figure expected to rise to about nine billion by 2050, and every single one of us needs resources – water, sunshine, space to live in, food, clothing and shelter. Access to natural resources matters to everyone; we all have a stake in the issues discussed in this book.

Resources are also implicated in some of the most serious potential challenges to our international order. As a result both of changes in technology and of global warming, areas that were undeveloped are now coming into focus – both by states, eager to extend their jurisdiction, and by multinational corporations, looking for new opportunities. Consider, for example, the various claims that have been made for control over the resources in the

Arctic, the ocean, the seabed, uninhabited islands and Antarctica. How, for example, ought we to assess the rival claims made by states in the South China Sea, which are disputed by China, Malaysia, Philippines and Taiwan? Or the dispute between Japan and South Korea over a chain of uninhabited islands and the adjacent seabed? Or the Arctic, which is the site of overlapping claims by Russia, Canada, the United States and Denmark? What kinds of claims make sense? We urgently need a conversation about who owns and who controls these natural resources and the terms in which we should interact with them, before we have developed the technology to harvest the resources contained therein. As it is, the profusion of claims and counter-claims are fuelled by the belief that the ocean bed and the Arctic and other uninhabited areas are rich in resources, and that gaining territory over these areas will enable the country to gain control over the resources.

Conflicts over resources do not just occur at the international level. They are also a feature in the domestic politics of almost every state. Consider the dispute over building an oil pipeline in British Columbia, which has been backed by Alberta, where much of the oil is produced, but has met stiff opposition from aboriginal groups and their supporters, who have objected to the pipeline going through aboriginal land. Or consider the conflict between pastoralists and agriculturalists in many parts of Africa, which is primarily about access to arable land and water resources. This conflict has been exacerbated by recent development projects aimed at irrigating some farmland and controlling flooding, which has had the effect of jeopardizing access to vital land and water for pastoralist herders, and thereby upsetting previously arrived-at understandings of how the two groups can co-exist in the same geographical area. Or consider the destruction of the rainforest in places like Borneo, which has been fuelled by landowners planting palm oil trees for international markets, but which are detrimental to the interests of future generations of people, who will almost certainly experience the harmful effects of human-induced climate change, which rainforests help to mitigate.

At present, we lack a general theory to examine our relationship to resources, and we therefore find it difficult to address specific cases of resource conflict. As a result, we have very fractured intuitions about rival claims. This may not be apparent from the example above, where the claims of the greedy plantation owner are pitted against the overall health of the planet, but what about when we add the idea that many of the world's poor rely on cheap palm oil as an important source of food? Or – to make the point more directly – how do we feel about the resource claims made in a place such as Brazil, between the poor, who argue that their poverty should be addressed through accessing the rich natural resources of the Amazon, and those of Amazonian indigenous people, who are living on huge swathes of the Amazonian jungle, and who resist development there. In many cases, we are sympathetic to both kinds of claims, and are unsure how to resolve such conflicts.[1]

What we need, I argue in this book, is a political theory of resource justice, which examines the varied nature of human beings' relationship to the natural world and thereby helps us to answer the question of what is at stake in any particular claim to a resource. Once we know what is at stake, we can formulate a normative analysis of resource justice, including the rights and duties that we have in relation to a particular resource (control of it, extraction rights and so on).

The question posed in the title of the book – who should own the world's natural resources? – is intended to be understood both more broadly than perhaps first appears, and more narrowly. It is narrower than it might be because the question is a normative one: it does not ask who now owns resources, but who *should* do so, or perhaps even more accurately, who should control, use and benefit from them. It is also intended to be understood more broadly, to encompass not only issues of ownership per se, by which I mean the rules of property ownership that are typically part of the laws of societies, but also issues of *jurisdiction* over resources by governments, as well as what justice requires that we leave for future generations. In order to answer these questions, I argue that we have to clarify what normatively is at stake in any claim to entitlement over resources – what kinds of entitlements individuals or communities might have to a resource, given their relationship to it; and the claims made by people to resources that they have never seen and which are far from where they live, both spatially and temporally.

To the extent that we have considered justice and natural resources, it is mainly as a component or part of a larger theory of distributive justice theory. I argue, however, that this is an unsatisfactory and truncated way to think about our relationship to the natural world. This book rejects the distributive paradigm, and offers instead a relational theory that examines how we, individually and in the groups that matter to us, are related to resources.

Some might think that the argument of this book echoes a complaint that libertarians have made against liberal theories of justice. Robert Nozick famously argued that theories of distributive justice treat goods as if they are *manna* from heaven, and fail to recognize that goods need to be produced, which gives rise to entitlements on the part of producers. However, this familiar argument suggests that natural resources are precisely the kind of thing that ought to be subject to distributive justice, because they are just there, not produced by anyone. This debate has, I think, occluded our view about the kind of relationship that we do have with respect to the natural world, and the resources in it, including land.

The relational theory of resource justice advanced in this book is both pluralist and contextual: pluralist because it offers more than one principle, and contextual because it does not offer a top-down theory which assesses claims in the abstract, but focuses instead on the claims that are made, and the relationship between the claimant and the land or resource in question, and proffers principles that provide guidance on how we are to assess them in the specific ways that they have emerged in cases of conflict. I adopt an approach similar to the one pioneered by Michael Walzer, who argued that different things can take on different meanings in different contexts and that it is important to know what the good is to the people in question. Walzer pointed out, for example, how 'bread' can have many different meanings – for some, it may refer to food or survival; for others, it could be religiously symbolic, such as 'holy eucharist' bread; or for still others, it may refer to a long-standing family business, or unique cultural symbol (such as bagels or German pretzels). Similarly, if we are to understand the value of land and of resources, we have to probe the specific ways in which people interact with resources and land, the meaning that these things have for them, and then consider how, when conflicts arise, they can be resolved or at least mitigated.

Definitions

The relational approach to resource justice begins with the very way in which we conceive of what is a natural resource. I regard natural resources as things that are derived from the environment and not made by humans, while being related in some way to human purposes and conceptions. This is a very open definition of natural resources as part of the 'natural wealth' of the world: land, water, air and sunshine are natural resources, as well as plants, animals and mineral ores. A hiking area is a resource; so too is a sacred mountain. Although natural resources have a physical character – as oil or coal or firewood or plant life – they are transformed into *resources* by being important for human purposes and this relational character explains how we individuate resources. This means that what counts as a resource is historically, culturally and individually variable. Different people will individuate resources differently: in the case of a tree, if what matters to one person is the bark; to someone else, the leaves; and someone else, the wood, then that counts as three different resources. If another person needs the whole tree, then that person considers the tree as a resource.[2] What this means of course is that something can be a resource for one person or one group, but not a resource for someone else.

This relational conception allows us to have a more capacious understanding of our relationship to the natural world than the usual one, where resources are conceived of as related to us purely instrumentally, as 'resources' for us to use. So in this book I emphasize the non-instrumental ways in which we are related to the natural world, where the language of 'resource' is perhaps itself too suggestive of the idea that they are only important as inputs to human welfare. I want to resist this thought, as I think that there are many different reasons why people care about the natural world and its resources, including land. They may care about it because it is historically significant in the life of the community with which the person identifies; or because it is sacred; or because the person grew up there, and her parents' ashes are spread there.

Aims, Argument and Structure of the Book

In order to understand the motivation for writing this book, it is important to see the flaws in the current accounts of resources and theories of resource justice. In chapter 2, I lay out three prominent theories of resource justice in more detail and show what's wrong with them. I do accept at least two of the core principles that animate these accounts, but I reject their general approaches, both because they do not consider the full variety of normatively significant ways that we interact with resources and, relatedly, because they tend to assimilate the value of resources to whatever is important in the theory of distributive justice.

This brings me to the positive argument of the book. Given that there are many different kinds of resources,[3] which are implicated in different relations between people and the external world, a *normative* analysis requires that we examine how different people interact with resources, and what kind of interest is at stake that may give rise to a claim to use, access and/or control resources.[4] In chapter 3, I argue that we can identify at least five different ways in which humans interact with resources in ways that, it could be argued, give rise to a claim. Here I just label them, as follows:

(1) claims based on individual *consumption*, which gives rise to a claim based on *need*, which I cash out in the language of basic rights;

(2) claims based on individual *production*, which give rise to a *desert-based claim* under justified rules;

(3) claims to individual and collective access or use of resources, which I examine in terms of the language of *legitimate expectations*;

(4) community claims to exercise *jurisdictional authority* over resources and land, broadly speaking in the geographical area that the community lives in, which is justified on the basis of *collective self-determination*; and

(5) claims to non-extraction and protection, which arise from the (presumed) interests or basic rights of future generations.

Some of the claims I will discuss are claims for *jurisdiction* – that is, claims directed at who (or what institution or group) is entitled to exercise control in making rules about resources; whereas other claims are primarily property-type claims, which are connected to what individual or collective is entitled to own property. Some theorists view property as foundational: they offer an account that explains how individuals acquire property and then this account helps to explain how the state acquires jurisdictional authority, which is necessary primarily to protect property.[5] Others tend to take the opposite view. They regard jurisdiction as primary: it is the political order that creates the rules of acquisition, transfer, bequest and so on that we associate with property rights.[6] Although the distinction between jurisdiction and property and the precise relationship between them is important, I sidestep this question.

The central focus in the discussion of the five different types of claims is on the justificatory argument that is used to support the claim. By examining the relationship between the claim to the resource and the argument that is used to ground the entitlement, it is possible, I argue, to assess the strength and limitations of the various claims. The first two – needs and desert – are argued for as the positive upshot of chapter 2; and the other three are the heart of the argument of chapter 3.

It would hardly be satisfactory, however, if I developed a pluralist account of resources without saying anything about what to do when these various claims conflict or the limitations of each of the claims. This is the aim of chapter 4. I also argue that which level of jurisdiction should apply depends on the kind of resource we are considering, and especially the relationship between human beings and the resources. In chapter 5, as an extension of the question of resource conflict, I consider the claims of future generations which may come into conflict with the claims of the present generation. This last chapter is addressed to the question: what (resources) do we owe the future generation? In answering that question, I also question the usual assumptions of theorists of intergenerational justice, who rely on a conception of a basket of substitutable resources that should be passed on to the next generation.

A central, perhaps unifying, thought in the chapters that follow is that at least some natural resources feature in people's lives such that they can't be substituted for other things – for money, or shares, or goods made by humans and so on. My claim is that this is so in part because of the way the natural world features in people's life plans, such that (at least sometimes) they can't be substituted. The people of Kiribati, a small group of Pacific islands which are under threat by rising oceans caused by human-induced global climate change, can be offered more money, stocks and shares or a different place to live if their island home disappears, but my intuition is that this doesn't really amount to true compensation. Compensation may be part of what could be done for such people in the event that they lose their island home. But this shouldn't blind us to the fact that what we have here is an absolute loss; for the Kiribati islanders, who will no longer be able to visit the places where they grew up, where their ancestors are buried, or smell the particular smell of the rainforest in the wet season; and also – though I do not fully make good this claim – for the world.[7] It is this thought which leads me to reject the current dominant theories of justice and resources, and to defend a pluralist and contextual theory that focuses on our many different relationships to things in the natural world.

2

Theories of Resource Justice

One answer to the question, 'Who ought to own the world's natural resources?' is: everyone. The resources of the world should not be in the control of a single state, benefitting only the citizens of that state. Nor should they be appropriated by a small minority of the world's population – the rich – for their sole benefit. Both scenarios would allow rich political communities, and rich people within those communities, or rich people in the world, to 'hog' the resources for themselves. This is unjustifiable, so the argument goes, because natural resources themselves are unequally distributed across the face of the earth, and no one is responsible for creating them.

For the reason given, many conclude that all human beings have some form of equal entitlement to the world's natural resources. This thought is implicit in the theories – equal common ownership, equal rights to private ownership and equal welfare theories – discussed in this chapter. Although, as will become clear, I share many of the same intuitions, and even embrace some elements of their conclusions, in this chapter I lay out the basic positions, and then discuss what is wrong with them, focusing on a wider difficulty in the way that they view the relationship between human beings and the natural world.

Equal Common Ownership

Ownership is a relationship between persons and external objects, such as land and moveable things like clothes and tools and furniture, and natural things like metal or wood or animals. Ownership can come in different forms, depending on what kinds of liberties, powers, claims and immunities are built into the idea of 'owning' something. This is because ownership is conceptualized as a bundle or cluster of constituent rights, which are logically separable and often separated in different kinds of property systems.[1] Among the most commonly distinguished 'incidents' of 'full liberal ownership' are the rights to use a thing, to alienate it, to exclude others from using it and non-expropriation of it. Obviously since ownership has various different elements, the idea of common ownership needs to be further specified.

To what does the idea of *common ownership* refer? This is a moral conception that involves two fundamental ideas: (1) the idea of equal status, and (2) the idea that we are dependent for our lives on access to external objects ('the fruits of the earth'). Equality is important to the theory: the various common ownership views may have differences, but they all endorse a symmetrical relationship or status of all individuals with regard to resources, and resources themselves are viewed in an undifferentiated way, at least at the initial stage of the argument.

There are different ideas of what it means to be co-owners on common land.[2] The term evokes the image of a group of people living around an area of land that they use in common. We can imagine a common area that is a free-for-all. Everyone could choose to walk on the land, to play games on it, run sheep or cattle or goats on it, dig up some of the earth and plant potatoes and vegetables. However, we can also imagine problems with this.

One problem might be that there is little incentive for any particular person to invest their time and effort in developing the land to improve its productivity. Since the land is common, there is no way for an individual to ensure that she will benefit from her investment because the prospective investor cannot exclude free-riders from reaping the rewards without contributing to the labour. Moreover, the problem isn't simply an incentive one: it may be rational to deplete the resources, to prevent other less scrupulous people from getting there first. In the last 50 years, we have witnessed our own version of the tragedy of the commons with respect to over-fishing in the oceans, which is a kind of commons. For more than 300 years, Newfoundland fishing communities in small outports dotted along the coast of the island relied on the cod fishery to sustain their way of life. Every fisher had a strong reason to conserve fish stocks, but the problem in an unregulated and unowned environment is that, if I take only my own, sustainable portion of fish, I will be leaving the fish for others to take. Indeed, with the advent of big factory fishing trawlers, equipped with advanced sonar and fish tracking devices, when the small Newfoundland fisher restricted her share of the fish catch, in line with some idea of sustainability, she succeeded only in leaving them for some other, Spanish or Russian or Japanese trawlers. The result was that, by 1992, when a Moratorium on

Fishing was finally declared, the ecological disaster had already happened: the fishers of Newfoundland, who had relied on the cod fishery for more than 300 years, were unemployed, their way of life destroyed, and the fish all gone. While many different groups of people had a compelling interest in sustaining those stocks, and that way of life, the relationship of each of the interested parties with respect to the ocean meant that it was individually rational to take as much cod as one could catch. Any theory of resource justice has to reflect on this story and the possible solution to it. As I will argue below, one solution to such tragedies, especially when they operate over land or divisible resources, is to privatize the resource, so that each person has an incentive to manage her own land or stock. But another solution, over a resource like the oceans, is to have a jurisdictional authority that can enforce rules over such places. Which of these solutions makes sense depends on the resource and our relation to it. But jurisdiction – coercively enforced rules by a legitimate authority – is at least part of the solution here, as I will argue in chapter 3.

A second problem with the common ownership view is that of resource use incompatibility. Imagine that you and others like you have goats to produce milk and cheese and eventually meat. I plant vegetables. Your goats eat all my vegetables. This can also lead to the tragedy of the commons, where the common land under-produces goods relative to other systems of land-holding. But the source here is not overuse, but potential resource conflict. (However, it would seem that repeated attacks by goats would also lead to under-investment which would also lead to the tragedy of the commons.)

To overcome these problems, the commoners might agree that each of them could use the land as they want, provided that it was consistent with others' uses, and 'consistent with' could be ensured by giving each co-owner a veto over the others' uses. This is a form of joint ownership.[3] The problem with this, though, is that the use (or division) of the resources of the world can't depend upon unanimous consent, because we would never be able to obtain such consent; contrary people in the group could wilfully prevent others from using the land, and therefore the people will starve. Veto rights also run against the idea of liberty: part of the point of ownership, presumably, is that people have liberty rights in the external world. But if these rights depend on the consent of others, as it would be with this way of conceiving of the commons, people wouldn't be autonomous at all, but restricted by the decisions and wilfulness of other people.

Perhaps, though, the group of people could find a different solution to the problems that arise in the commons. This solution involves departing from common ownership and accepting some system of private property. This was argued initially by John Locke, but is central to current liberal theories of resource ownership and property. It is to this account that I now turn.

Equal Rights and Private Ownership

One of the central questions that preoccupied early liberal theorists was: how can private property rightfully emerge from what is naturally common? John Locke and his heirs recognize that, in some sense, the world and all contained therein (land, water, moveable natural resources) were not originally divided up into state territory or individual private property holdings. They were in some sense 'held in common' but liberals argued that the deficiencies of common ownership were such that it justified private property acquisition and state rules to enforce property rules and natural rights.

To see the liberal argument regarding the deficiencies of common ownership, let's return to the problem of resource use incompatibility. Instead of telling the prospective goat-owner that she cannot have a goat, perhaps the solution is to permit the vegetable-grower to take a piece of land and build a fence around it, so that she can grow her own vegetables on her own piece of land without requiring your permission. That would definitely solve the goat–vegetable problem (and would also solve some types of over-use problems, such as over-grazing on the commons), but might give rise to other sorts of problems.

Suppose that the piece of land that the vegetable-grower decides to fence in is one that other people used to use. Perhaps they picked fruit or grazed their animals there, or accessed the river. But now that I've built a fence around it, the liberty that other people had to use the world is reduced. Indeed, it's not just that the scope of their liberty is reduced: it's that the rights that they enjoyed in the commons aren't very meaningful if they can be extinguished in a purely unilateral manner.[4] How can we think of this as a justified form of ownership, rooted in the value of human liberty, if other people's actions can extinguish the co-owner's rights without her consent? That is problematic in itself, but perhaps especially problematic in cases where everyone appropriates some land, and leaves someone without any land at all. Consider the case of someone who goes away all summer, grazing his flock of goats on higher pastures, and finds, when he returns, that all the land is privatized, and there is none left at all, for him, for his goats, to build his hut, and so on? This seems doubly unjust.

To guard against that possibility, it might be argued that each commoner is entitled to appropriate the commons (to solve the goat attacking vegetables, investment incentive and other similar problems) *as long as they leave enough for others*. This is attractive in some ways, because it doesn't hold people hostage to the consent of others, as does the joint ownership conception, and it also ensures that no one is left without any land at all. On this view, associated with the work of Hillel Steiner, one can rightfully appropriate one's share of private land or resources without the consent of other commoners. However, this means that, once the population grows so large that it is not possible to leave others with equal shares, they must either downsize or pay compensation to those who are excluded or do not have equivalent shares. The problem with downsizing – which is perhaps an obvious solution for an equality theory with increased population and static natural resources – is that it fails to provide security of possession, which property rights promise to do, and

22

which is key to solving other problems, such as under-investment. Steiner's own preferred solution is compensation. By the term 'compensation', I mean that the person is given something else of a certain value but not the thing itself. This is usually thought to be equivalent to the value of the thing lost or in addition to the value, to make good the suffering that one has endured by the loss of the original thing. One difficulty with compensation is that the excluded may not want compensation: they might want to be included. Suppose you take a very beautiful, fertile piece of land, which I grew up near, and to which I am attached. I would rather have the land than the compensation for its value. So it might seem that the theory still doesn't treat the excluded properly; indeed, we might (as I will argue at length below) question the assumption that all land and all resources can be compensated.

Moreover, compensation on this theory is only for the value of the appropriated *unimproved* natural resources, but not the improvements that the labourer may have added to the thing. This is because the labourer is entitled to the additional value, and it would be wrong to take this. This leads to a further difficulty: that of measuring the value of natural resources which owners have taken with them, and therefore what non-owners are entitled to by way of compensation. It is not immediately clear how we can distinguish between the value that inheres in a thing naturally, and therefore cannot be deserved, and the value that is human-created. Although sometimes we can identify the value of a piece of land before and then after some human improvement (before and after fertilizing it, or before and after irrigating it), in many cases, the value of a piece of land is inextricably linked, not with specific acts of improvement, but with proximity to other places of human creation – proximity to cafes, restaurants, theatres, shopping and so on.[5] This fact has to be recognized: if it were not, it would mean that someone who appropriated some fertile field in North Dakota should pay compensation to someone who owns a block of less fertile but vastly more valuable (in market terms) land in the centre of Tokyo. Alternatively, if we rely on market value, we incorporate into our conception of the value of natural resources many things that are the product of human decisions and endeavours, especially including decisions that we have made collectively, about the rules of regulation and transfer of land, which is not justified by the common ownership of the natural resources of the earth conception.

In what follows, though, I will raise concerns not

about the potential exclusion of non-appropriators nor the specific account of what it means to hold things in common nor how to measure value, though these are serious difficulties that this view doesn't come to grips with adequately. I will focus on the problems with the underlying idea of ownership itself; the conception of resources at its heart; and especially the univocal view of the relationship of human beings to the world.

The Problem with Ownership, Resources and the Instrumentalizing Gaze

Theorists in both the common and private ownership traditions describe our relation to the natural world in the language of 'resources', a term which they use in a very instrumental and generic way. The reason why exclusion is problematic is said to be that it is exclusion from *resources*, which have uses to people, and which people need. The idea that people can be *compensated* for exclusion from resources, which is explicit in Steiner's argument, but implicit in all of them, suggests a homogeneous and undifferentiated view of resources as existing in the world, important to meeting human needs (for food, shelter and wealth creation, for example) and thereby raising questions of property and distributive justice. Exclusion from natural resources can be compensated by increased goods of other kinds – money, shares, human-made things, which suggests that resources are related to human beings in a purely instrumental way, and are potentially exchangeable or substitutable.

The conception of resources adopted by proponents of this view is, of course, not the one advanced in chapter 1, where I argued that, although natural resources are indeed (a) derived from the environment, and (b) not made by humans, they also (c) contain an important relational element, so that the individuation function (to individuate resources) is done in relation to human intentionality. This means that it's wrong, even as a conception of resources, to view them as undifferentiated, potentially substitutable 'stuff'. It matters how they are related to human beings.

Some resources of course are generic and substitutable and the claims of human need are probably compellingly described in terms of access to water, or food or shelter, but not access to a particular river or particular type of dinner or the particular house that I was born in. What I am disputing is that all of our legitimate claims with respect to the natural world can be described in generic terms.

And, perhaps just as pressingly, why do we discuss our relationship to the external world in terms of *ownership* at all? The idea of owning the world suggests that the world or nature is at the disposal of humans; that we have rights with respect to resources – indeed, that the natural world is a resource for us. But it's not clear what kinds of duties we have with respect to it. There are of course different legal relations that could characterize ownership, some more or less permissive, but the underlying thought is that the thing owned is at the disposal of the owner: it is the owner individually or collectively that has rights with respect to the thing. To be sure, on this view, no human being has a privileged claim vis-à-vis one another, but it seems that the concept of ownership comes with the idea of the owner having rights (liberty rights, powers, etc.) with respect to the thing. What is ruled out from the start are various different kinds of ways of interacting with the external world, which may have normative significance, but which seem not to be captured in the relationship of ownership. These are not merely activities of individual and collective consumption and production, which can produce different kinds of goods (individualized private property, collective goods, pure public goods) but also non-subtractive use, such as hiking in a forest or artistic appreciation of the beauty of a landscape, as well as a community's reliance interest in a particular place or particular habitat to sustain a particular way of life. As I will argue in the next chapter, not all of these relationships between human beings and the world can properly be described as *ownership*, though they may give rise to normatively significant entitlements and obligations; and that we figure out these entitlements and obligations – alienation, deriving income, rights of management or regulation, exclusion – by examining the economic, cultural, symbolic and other relations between human beings, both individual and collective, and the world that we live in.

Equality of Welfare, Opportunities for Welfare and Armstrong's Theory of Resource Justice

Let us turn to another egalitarian framework for resource justice: a version of welfare egalitarianism, or equal opportunity for welfare, which incorporates resources as a component or driver of welfare.

One promise of a welfarist position with respect to resources is that it does not deploy the problematic concept of ownership, with its suggestion of a uniform relationship of owner to the things in the world. Rather, on this view, what matters for equality is equal welfare, and different people can get welfare from different sources. Indigenous people in a Bornean rainforest are related to the external world differently than the Bornean plantation owner residing in Kuala Lumpur; and an equality of welfare conception can incorporate both kinds of claims. By leaving open the precise relationship between individuals and communities to the external world, this theory promises to be able to incorporate diverse conceptions of people's relationship to resources, and the goods that are thereby realized, while explaining the limits of each person's claims, in egalitarian terms.[6]

Welfare egalitarianism also holds out the promise of being able to incorporate attachment claims, which means that it is able to appreciate the ways in which particular people are related in normatively significant ways to particular places or to particular resources. If it can do so, it would represent a significant advance over other egalitarian theories. This is because it would be counter-intuitive if it couldn't incorporate this sort of claim: after all, attachment to place (to land or to place) is the underlying idea behind the basic human right not to be expelled from one's land or country, and the right of return that people who have been expelled also have and which is recognized by international law; and also underlying indigenous people's claims to particular lands, which is accepted in the United Nations Declaration on the Rights of Indigenous Peoples.

In what way, then, does this sort of theory 'accommodate' attachment claims? First, as a welfarist theory, it takes seriously that people can get welfare from different sources, and this in itself seems to give some credence to the idea that some people – or some groups – would get welfare from particular activities in particular places and that this would be inputted into the theory. Further, it could be argued that many of the groups that make these sorts of claims and for whom we feel the most sympathy – indigenous people, for example – are themselves relatively marginalized. So, accommodating these sorts of claims might be exactly what an egalitarian theory ought to do: it can grant such claims without jeopardizing equality, because the claim is only for certain kinds of rights to certain very particular kinds of resources, which can be granted without jeopardizing equality of opportunity for welfare. On this view, resources matter, not in themselves, but because 'they are an important fuel for well-being and when possible we ought to seek to channel their benefits so as to promote more equal access to well-being for all the world's individuals'.[7]

There are two types of problem with this kind of approach – one conceptual and the other, more directly related to whether this type of theory can realize the two advantages outlined above. First, there's the conceptual issue. Most welfarist theories do not try to equalize welfare itself. Since some people have lots of opportunities but just don't do what is necessary to convert these opportunities into their own flourishing, most forms of equality of welfare focus on whether people are provided with equal *opportunities for welfare*. The metric of justice – that whose distribution we ought to care about in order to realize justice – is *opportunity for welfare*.[8] It is crucial, however, that an equal opportunity for welfare theory should be able to determine when two qualitatively different opportunity sets are equal in value, which is notoriously difficult to do when heterogeneous resources are involved. The most prominent recent welfarist theory of resource justice does not even attempt to do this, but operates instead entirely through intuitive examples, arguing that we ought to favour moves that are 'equalizing' or 'equality-promoting' without explaining how we know when a 'move' is indeed equalizing.[9]

Second, how well does such a theory accommodate attachment claims? It could be argued that not all special claims will disrupt equality, because often the claimants are themselves relatively marginalized, and granting them could be consistent with global welfare equality. An equal opportunity for welfare theory could grant 'special' or exceptional claims, especially if these are relatively costless and/or are claimed by a relatively marginalized group.

This is questionable however. Claims to particular resources are not made only by demographically insignificant groups, such as indigenous people, who resist the instrumentalization of the natural world as a resource. Although this is in part an empirical question, we should reflect on the vast amount of literature and art on the relationship between people and land – from the peasant farmer in China in Pearl S. Buck's *The Good Earth*, to Clara's fight against developers, who seek to remove her from her home, in the Brazilian film *Aquarius*. We should reflect, too, on people in fishing communities who are reliant on fish for their way of life, or people living in urban neighbourhoods, who are resisting expulsion and gentrification processes, to see that many different individuals and communities have non-instrumental relationships to land and to place.

Contrary to the assumption that such demands can be granted consistent with equality, I would argue that many of these claims can be quite costly. Even the Sámi, who are a relatively small, indigenous population in Scandinavia, have claimed special rights vis-à-vis the states (Sweden, Norway, Finland) where they live and the majority population there. They do not seek only a right to unimpeded migration over their traditional territory, which can be accommodated consistent with other land use patterns (and whether they are indeed consistent with farming or managed forestry is much debated). They, along with most other indigenous peoples, and also national minorities and territorial peoples, are also claiming a right to exercise forms of collective self-determination over their lives, within a geographical space. If the Sámi are making claims to a traditional territory, in which they herd reindeer, then, for this to be effective, they have to restrict other uses of the land that may be incompatible with herding migratory animals. This may well be very costly indeed, particularly if the area is found to be rich in some kind of resource that is useful to other individuals but whose extraction is incompatible with the Sámi's traditional way of life.

This does not, of course, show that equality of welfare is wrong or that the Sámi claims are indefensible. What it does show, however, is that this theory resembles the common ownership view in its reliance on a single univocal view of resources, though conceived of as drivers for welfare; and is problematic for the same reason. It also does not really make good the promise of being able to accommodate special claims, but can only do so when those claims happen to coincide with the overall goal of global equality of opportunities for welfare, which, I've argued, is unlikely, and which fails to incorporate the claims in their own, normatively compelling terms.

In summary, I believe that this approach is deeply flawed, and that we should begin, not by assuming equality vis-à-vis resources, but with the assumption that, by virtue of being born or having lived in specific places, we develop attachments and connections to people in these places and with the places themselves. It would be hugely disruptive, to our plans, ways of life and relationships, to be disconnected from the land on which we live, the place(s) that we have made home and the resources that are central to our way of life. We might feel their loss deeply, and their deprivation would probably be perceived (rightly) as a form of injustice, precisely because the claim of a person whose life is intertwined with a particular place or particular resource is more powerful than the claim of someone who is unconnected; which would make the equality principle with respect to that resource, deeply unfair. What we need, I argue next, is a more complex theory, which examines the diverse ways in which people are related to land and to particular resources.

Production and Consumption: Desert under Justified Rules and Claims based on Human Needs

Both common ownership and equality of opportunity for welfare theories, which I've just examined, point to two ways in which human beings are related to resources that generate justified claims (or rights): we are related to things through *production* and *consumption*. The liberal argument stemming from Locke posited, among other things, that the activity of production gives rise to normative claims. This may be conceptualized as a fundamental moral claim to entitlement to the fruits of one's labour, rooted in individual freedom, or the view that humans have entitlement to meet their needs through interacting with resources, which gives rise to a property claim. I leave open, at least here, what substantively is involved in a justified rule to regulate production, except to say that I assume that some rules may be unjustified, and that it's unlikely that there is one particular uniquely justified set of rules.

Both common ownership and equality of opportunity for welfare theories also conceive of human beings as related to resources through the activity of *consumption*. Lockean theories emphasize needs and equality of welfare theories emphasize the relationship between resources, consumption and welfare. We do not need to accept the language of common ownership to endorse the idea that human *need* can generate entitlements to (some) resources. Consider the language of basic rights pioneered by Henry Shue in his book *Basic Rights: Subsistence, Affluence and U.S. Foreign Policy*. There are deep disagreements about how to distinguish the list of what we might think of as 'human rights' from other moral rights. I do not attempt to do this here, but, following Shue, I accept that, whatever the conception of human rights we have, and whatever the list of human rights we adopt, it should at the minimum include 'basic rights', by which Shue meant those rights – to physical security and subsistence – that are necessary to other rights. In his discussion of the minimum reasonable demand that we associate with subsistence rights, Shue discusses some resources – unpolluted air, unpolluted water, adequate food, adequate shelter – and some minimum of preventative health care.[10] I take 'need' (by which I mean to reference Shue's subsistence right and his list of associated resources) as an unproblematic principle of individual resource entitlement.

Of course, humans consume much more than we actually need. Can consumption beyond what we need for subsistence generate entitlements? I think it is hard to explain why people (as consumers) would be *entitled* to more than they need, because it is difficult to explain why others are under a duty to guarantee them support that they don't need, but perhaps would like. It is possible, though, to appeal to other normative considerations beyond need. Imagine, for example, that we live in a world called Cornucopia, which harnesses an environmentally friendly form of energy, such as solar power, and is wealthy enough that it can provide generously for everyone.[11] In this scenario, it might be claimed, mere subsistence is inadequate because almost everyone else is better off than the person who is only able to meet basic needs. I agree that, in this context, basic subsistence to meet physical needs is inadequate. However, this just shows that the conditions for a flourishing life, which gives content to our conception of what is required as a 'basic right', should incorporate what is needed in the society in question. The idea here is that the concept of 'need' is not invariant, because different societies will have different thresholds of resources to meet the conditions for self-respect and relational equality. This argument doesn't challenge the idea of basic subsistence rights, but, rather, is a helpful corrective: it suggests that a sophisticated account of subsistence rights should incorporate the idea of social variability and the importance of conditions for relational equality. Other forms of entitlement to resources, which I will discuss in the next chapter, don't explicitly frame the argument in terms of need.

Conclusion

In this chapter I have argued that the dominant theories of resource justice share the same problematic view of resources as essentially undifferentiated – as either purely instrumental to human needs or drivers for human welfare, which can be compensated by other ways of realizing needs and welfare. I have criticized these views as offering a truncated view of the diverse ways in which people are related to natural resources, to land, to place and to the natural world. In the next chapter I discuss some claims in which the *particular* place is important to people's life plans and can't be substituted for some other place. In these cases, it might be necessary, as a second-best principle of corrective justice, to have principles of compensation to offset loss, but we should not view the person as fully *compensated*. This is because there are many different ways in which individuals and communities are related to place, to land and to the natural world, and some of these relations may have non-instrumental value.

3

Resources and People: A Pluralist Relational Approach

Thus far, I have discussed human beings' relationships with the natural world in the language of consumption and production. The arguments discussed in the previous chapter, which justified subsistence rights and entitlement under the rules of property, applied principally to generic resources. By generic resources, I mean resources that are potentially substitutable. The right to food is not a right to a specific kind of dinner but to food in general, which can be met in different ways. Arguments related to production can and do generate rights to the thing produced, which is normally discussed in terms of the additional value that is created through the process of interacting with the resource. In this chapter I elaborate on some of the other ways that we individually and collectively interact with land and resources so as to give rise to claims over them, and most of these claims are to specific places or specific resources. I do not here discuss what to do when these different kinds of claims conflict – chapter 4 is devoted to that problem – but focus instead on the conditions under which a person or group can claim rights to specific resources based on a relationship that she or they have to the thing in question.

In the first half of the chapter I discuss the idea of legitimate expectations, which I understand capaciously, to include what might be thought of as 'cultural' claims by communities, as well as more standard historical claims based on past reliance on the land or resource by individuals and affected groups. In the second half, I discuss the argument for a community's claim to exercise jurisdictional authority over a particular geographical area and, connected to this, for rights of control over resources. Both kinds of argument challenge the assumptions that we are all equally situated with respect to natural resources, and that the loss of some natural resource can be compensated by gains on another dimension.

Some of the arguments contained in this chapter have been discussed by critics under the rubric 'attachment theory'. However, this wrongly implies that there is some kind of general, overarching attachment 'theory' of justice in resources. This assumption is incorrect: I argue below that there are a number of different kinds of claims, with different strengths, which do justify some forms of entitlement, but it's necessary to specify what precisely is claimed, and how this can justify the duty in question.

Legitimate Expectations and Resources

One of the most common types of arguments for why an individual might be entitled to a *particular* good and/or could be entitled to more than would be justified by a needs-based argument proceeds by stressing that the person has become used to a certain lifestyle, and that they are 'attached' to a particular set of resources. This is at least one aspect of what Armstrong and Ypi think 'attachment theorists' argue in relation to claims to resources.[1] As I will argue below, this is too simplistic: we need to disaggregate different sorts of claims and entitlements.

Let's begin with one sort of claim, which is sometimes treated as a form of 'attachment': this is a claim based on subjective affection for a particular place or resource. This emotional response to place

is not unusual: people are sometimes deeply connected to particular places, to land that they farmed
and was passed down from their father or mother
or the house that they grew up in. This is clearly
a powerful emotion, which has some force; and it
certainly raises problems for the generic account of
resources. However, it is a weak claim of entitlement in the sense that it may give one a stronger
claim to a thing than that of someone with no tie,
but it is difficult to generate strong claim rights
from this argument. This is in part because people
can develop emotional attachments for many different kinds of reasons and in part because it's
difficult to argue that people *are owed* the object
of their attachment. This sort of claim needs to be
buttressed with other claims, which explicate the
historical relationship that gave rise to the emotional response. This argument strengthens claims
that have merit for other reasons – most people
who are subjectively attached to, say, a family farm
also rely on it for their jobs or their way of life. But
on its own, emotional attachment doesn't generate
rights because X does not have a duty to provide Y
with something just because Y has affection for it.
On the other hand, the fact that people have these
emotional responses, these attachments, also means
that the loss of, say, a family farm can be a serious

loss, which can't be replaced fully by compensation with other things that are of the same value, such as human-made things or other kinds of opportunities, or stocks and shares. These can, of course, help psychologically to cope with the loss by thinking of other aspects of one's life, rather as the person who has just lost a child tries to cope with that loss by focusing on other reasons why she should live, such as her other children. But this in no way means that the loss itself is *compensated*.

Another argument that is sometimes treated as an 'attachment' form of argument emphasizes the importance of security of access to a particular good or a particular resource in making forward-looking plans and having projects and relationships, conceived of as extending into the future. It might then be claimed that this can generate entitlement to these particular resources, in addition to the generic resources that the basic rights argument can generate. Both Ypi and Armstrong view this sort of argument as the paradigm case of 'attachment theory' and they also provide examples that seem to undermine the moral force of such an argument. They pose the example of a very rich person, who is accustomed to living in a large mansion, with extensive woods and fields. Does this person have entitlement to this large property, independent of the property right that he or she may have? And, if so, doesn't the legitimate expectation argument have the counter-intuitive consequence that it justifies unfair allocations simply on the grounds of what people have come to expect?

In order to see what is wrong with this analogy, it is necessary to unpack what precisely a legitimate expectations argument can claim, and the extent to which it can generate duties. To do this, we need to consider what is meant by the term 'legitimate expectation'. It means, first, an expectation that is *reasonable* – it satisfies the epistemological condition of being something that we expect will happen in the future, for which there are good grounds. Expectations are necessary if we are to navigate the social world. These expectations arise from the operation of rules, practices, policies, norms and conventions that operate as the backdrop of the person's life, and so are not purely subjective. The concept is also a partly moralized concept – to be a *legitimate* expectation, it cannot be contrary to objective justice.[2] Nevertheless, there are many laws, practices and social conventions that are permissible – neither required by deeper justice nor egregiously unjust – and rules, practices and conventions of this sort are the subject of legitimate expectations.

How does this argument generate duties on others to provide people with what they expect? It can't be the simple fact that they expect things: after all, some people have very high expectations and others have low expectations but it's hard to see why this, in itself, would generate a duty on the part of other people to provide them with the object of their expectation. Rather, the central reason why there may be a duty is that individuals have been induced to rely on continued access to and/or use of a particular land or resource, and it would be *unfair* to that individual if the system changed suddenly. The duty is normally held by the person or institution that induced that reliance.[3] The harm to the individual person is not simply that of frustrated expectations, but the denial of a resource on which the person has reason to assume is a stable background context of her life, and use or possession of which is not contrary to justice or morality and in which a sudden change in policy and/or denial of a particular resource would be very disruptive to people's plans and interests, indeed, the goals and aspirations that may be central to her way of life.

Consider, as an example, the situation of an individual in a society that relies on two school systems for entrance to university: A levels and International

Baccalaureate (IB). Suppose either is fine – neither is required nor to be preferred from the standpoint of justice. But it would be wrong if the state suddenly changes its policies and decides that students who have studied under the IB system will no longer be recognized for university admissions. This seems unfair: the students had developed reliance interests in the stability of the practice; they have spent long hours studying in their schools and doing home-work to achieve the right grades for admission. It is this that justifies, at the minimum, that the individuals harmed by the sudden change in rules would be 'grandfathered', by which I mean that the rules would not apply to people who had entered their high-school stream under the old set of rules. In other cases, where 'grandfathering' is not pos-sible, compensation might be in order, and the duty (to compensate) would be owed by the party that generated the reliance interest.

How might this argument work in the case of resources? Consider the situation of many com-munities in south-west Texas, which are at the epicentre of the growth of new oil and gas drilling, which involves pumping large amounts of water, mixed with a chemical cocktail, to release oil and gas from the shale rock. Hydraulic fracking requires access to huge amounts of water which are pumped into the shale; and it has been associated with severe water stress in California, New Mexico, Utah, Oklahoma, Colorado and Texas.[4] In 2010, the inhabitants of the small community of Barnhart, Texas, were unexpectedly faced with the fact that their water supply had run dry. Some farmers in this area relied on their own private wells (a special case, to be considered next), but for the townspeople of Barnhart, it was reasonably expected that their taxes would pay for the basic infrastructure that every community needs, and water, surely, is among them. The warning signs of the impending water crisis had been there – air bubbles in the water supply, sand coming out of the taps – but nevertheless many residents reportedly were shocked to find that one day, no water came out of their taps, their toilets didn't flush, they couldn't launder their clothes. In short, without water, their entire way of life, and the fate of their town, was in question. On my argument, the people of Barnhart, Texas, had reliance interests of the most fundamental kind in access to water. It wasn't just an interest in water as a generic resource (although of course water is also a generic resource), because it wouldn't have been good enough for the town to say that water was available elsewhere, and they were free to move. Their claim was against the town authorities which had induced reliance since water is a key responsibility of any local level of government. It is also reasonable to think that the town had further claims against the large oil and gas companies that were at least partially responsible for draining the aquifer, and more distant political authorities that had failed to protect the Barnhart townspeople's interests. (As it happens, the town did recognize this obligation and was subsequently able to revive an abandoned railway well, though this is thought to be only a temporary solution.[5])

These examples illustrate that these historical claims (under the rubric of legitimate expectations) have moral force, but that they are also limited in two ways. First, a legitimate expectation claim is often time-limited. In general, it doesn't generate *permanent* entitlement. Like the grandfathering rule in the case of school systems, the thought is that sudden changes generate unfairness, but social policies can (legitimately) change, as long as they insulate people from the unfairness associated with the change. Indeed, change may be required, especially in cases where the current situation is unjust. As societies enact policies to transition from a high carbon-emitting lifestyle to a lower one, there may be people who need help adjusting to the change in technology or way of life, and this is justified and appropriate, even though the change itself may be required by justice.[6] This might mean compensation or a grandfathering policy that permits change over time, such as with the UK government's announcement in 2018 that it intends to ban gas and diesel cars by 2040, and the long lead-time to that policy announcement is designed to insulate people from sudden unfairness, in line with concern about people's legitimate expectations.[7]

The second limitation of a legitimate expectations argument is that it is most clearly applicable when the party that has induced reliance is also the party responsible for the change in policy and practice. But this is not true in many cases. Consider the people of south-west Texas again, who have experienced an 800 per cent increase in oil and gas drilling in their area, with new fracking technology. Ranchers have had to reduce herds, because there is little water; farmers on cotton fields have lost their crops due to drought and the fact that the wells on which they used to rely have now gone dry, as a result of the general draining of the groundwater aquifer. The claims of such people are broadly similar to that of the Barnhart townspeople, but they have no similar legal recourse. Property rights in that part of Texas are normally surface rights, with no entitlement to what is under the ground. And under the legal Rule of Capture, landowners were not required to get a permit to drill a well. This meant that any landowner could pump as much water as she could beneficially use (including selling it to oil and gas companies) even when this caused her neighbour's well to go dry. What sort of claim did those people (who had to give up farming or ranching or indeed living in their house, due to lack of water) have?

As normally understood, a legal argument framed in terms of legitimate expectations does not apply to such people. But what is legally required and what is morally required can diverge. While the legal doctrine does not support such claims, it is unreasonable to assume that the ordinary citizen – rancher, cotton farmer, resident – would have this detailed familiarity with the legal rules and corporate activities that are at work. From the rancher's or cotton planter's perspective, his or her situation is the same as the townspeople of Barnhart, Texas. Their lives have been turned upside down by the oil and gas company practices, which should have been regulated and organized in ways that protected citizens' interests. Even if there is no legal recourse, these people had a moral right to have their interests protected, to have avenues of control over their collective lives (which I'll discuss below, under the

51

heading 'jurisdictional control') and their interests in stability and secure access to this vital resource protected. If the water is gone, perhaps compensation (value for their loss, and perhaps additional value for the displacement and suffering meanwhile) is in order; but ideally their claims, rooted in their existing relation to the land and to water, would have been respected from the beginning, and their interests considered in the overall policy with respect to water use and oil consumption.

This brings us close to a related argument: that of communal reliance on a resource, which I'll discuss below in terms of three different kinds of communities that make a claim on specific resources based on their relations to that resource, ranging from small voluntary communities to larger encompassing religious or national communities. First, let's consider small single-interest communities based on resource use. If communities are valuable as important sources of collective identity and the relations to which they give rise as valuable in themselves, does that generate a right to resources for those communities that have a non-encompassing relationship to a particular resource? Consider groups such as hiking societies or surfing clubs. To the extent that access to specific resources are integral to these communities, which themselves embody morally valuable relations of friendship or shared purpose, we might think that this represents a morally valuable way in which people interact with resources. I think that these kinds of communities, which are largely voluntary, do have a claim, but it's a weak one, rooted in the idea that the resource is necessary to a particular activity and that individuals and groups are therefore important stakeholders with respect to that resource. However, this claim is quite weak because, while the individual or group may have developed reasonable expectations of continued use and access, these are the result of past permissive practice, not an induced reliance by a particular individual or policy, so there is no (individual or collective) agent that has a duty to ensure that this claim is met. Moreover, while the group does have a claim to continued use and access, it is not that strong, because, while single-interest voluntary groups may be important to some people, their loss does not have the same disorienting effect on people's lives as the loss of a resource that is central to the community's way of life. This is because people are typically in numerous other relationships and involved in other activities and associations, or could become so. In addition, no one can expect that everything will stay the same: after all, human beings are agents, and so we ought to expect that humans will change the social and natural world that we live in.

Second, there are larger religious or national communities, for whom certain places are of deep symbolic significance. In this category are the Jewish and Muslim claims to Jerusalem, the Muslim claim to Mecca or the Serbian claim to Kosovo. Such groups don't view the place as a resource, that is, only instrumental to the satisfaction of individual or collective preference, or even purely as a geographical space in which self-government can occur. Rather, the land is infused with emotional significance that has a deep historical basis. According to Serbian nationalist mythology, for example, Kosovo is the 'cradle' of their nation. Serbs have fought for control over Kosovo (in 1999) while accepting, eight years previously, the secession of the much more prosperous, objectively desirable territory of Slovenia. The attachment is connected to the historical significance of Kosovo in Serb nationalist mythology, and particularly to the monasteries, ancient battlefields and Orthodox churches there. While I would argue that this gives Serbs individually and collectively a right of *access* to these places of significance, or even some kind of jurisdictional authority in a power-sharing arrangement, it does not confer any right of jurisdictional authority *over the people* who live in Kosovo. Similarly, Jerusalem has important emotional and symbolic significance for Jews and Muslims, and the instrumental 'bundle' of resources picture doesn't capture this. Rights to Jerusalem cannot be replaced by some other site of equal fertility or equivalent material resources. And again, while its sacred status may generate some rights to the place, particularly individual rights of access to sites of religious significance, and some collective (religious community) rights to power-sharing over significant sites, so that these sacred places can be governed in accordance with appropriate (religious) norms, it cannot be used to generate rights to the resources in the area (water, minerals, etc.) nor, by itself, to jurisdictional authority over the people who live there.

Finally, let's consider claims by more encompassing communities, in which there are relations of production in addition to consumption, and in which the way of life of the group is inextricably connected to access to a particular resource such as a river or a rainforest or a particular farming area. This does not depend on a specific claim of significance, as in the examples above; rather, people are entwined in numerous relations, and have a way of life that depends for its continued existence on access to the resource. Think here of the Canadian Inuit for whom seal hunting is a traditional activity, and central to their way of life, and who argued on that basis for an exemption from a ban on the killing of seals and the use of seal products. They have a very strong reliance interest on this particular resource, which has been assumed to be a stable background context for the members of that community, and removal of the resource would be profoundly disruptive to the whole community. However, in contrast to the legitimate expectations in law and as applied to individuals, it is the whole community's practices and norms that help to generate the assumed expectation. I would argue that the cattle herder or cotton farmer, discussed above, who found their way of life jeopardized by the draining of the aquifer on which they relied, also fall into this category; they are a class of persons who rely on the resource, and this reliance is generated through general social norms, practices and ways of life. It's not that a specific individual or institution induced reliance (on seals in the case of the Inuit or on the aquifer in the case of the Texan cotton farmer) through their policies or practices, but that whole communities of people are reliant on access or use of a particular resource, and the basis of the reliance is customary and generally accepted. Some might think that this is weaker than specifically induced reliance, and in some respects it is, because it's harder to specify the duty-bearer. On the other hand, it's clear that in many societies, long-standing practices and conventions have the same status as government policies and do generate reasonable expectations on which people rely to navigate their lives socially. Indeed, it could be argued that communal reliance is stronger than individual reliance, not because of the aggregation of individual interests, but because communities of people themselves generate intrinsic goods, which are connected to the intrinsic value of friendships, or relationships of love and affection. If such communities, which have intrinsic value, are dependent on access to a particular resource, then this generates a stronger (than individual) claim to that resource.

Ypi has criticized this last implication of 'attachment theory' by pressing on parallel examples. She argues that there is no difference in attachment between Inuit seal-hunting and aristocratic fox-hunting, which has been practised in England for some 300 years, and which, it is claimed by pro-hunting activists, is important to their way of life. This example is used to question the 'attachment' argument, by suggesting that it has counter-intuitive implications. She also claims that, if we think there is an intuitive difference between these cases, it's because one group is marginalized and suffers from structural injustice (and these exemptions can be seen as part of a remedial package), whereas in the other case, the individuals in question are generally privileged.[8] It's clear, however, that the fox-hunting aristocrat example misrepresents the way that collective legitimate expectations arguments of this type work. I agree that the English landed aristocracy should not be able to continue fox-hunting on grounds of legitimate expectations and if this was the implication of my argument, I would be worried. But it is not. While fox-hunting is a feature that we associate with being an aristocrat, it's possible to be an aristocrat without hunting foxes at all. It's not very plausible to think that hunting foxes 'structures' aristocrats' lives, gives meaning and value to their group practices, and that their way of life requires access to that resource. Rather, this is more like the weak single-interest community discussed above, which means that they may be one of a number of possible stakeholders in what happens to the land (over which they traditionally hunted foxes), and their claim is not very strong, because the activity in question is problematic on a number of grounds, and, as I argued above, the legitimate expectations argument assumes the permissibility of the activity in question. It is very doubtful that we can ever have a 'legitimate expectation' to inflict unnecessary cruelty on sentient animals.

A more genuine parallel to the Inuit seal hunter case is that of Canadian East Coast sealers and fishers, who also rely on hunting seals as a supplement to fishing. If we want to examine whether structural injustice is really key to our intuitions, we might consider that case: they are not privileged, but they are not victims of structural injustice either, at least as that is normally understood; and nor are they defined by group-based (racial, gender, sexual orientation or historical group) oppression. I think that those East Coast communities that genuinely rely on hunting seals have an important claim. It might – like the Inuit claim – be a defeasible one, but it seems that they can make a claim to continued access to that resource, as implicated in something of moral importance to them, for which they should at least be compensated if they are suddenly prevented from doing so (and to outweigh their claim, the reason would have to be a strong one, such as a reason of justice or stewardship of the environment).

Jurisdictional Authority over Resources

Let me turn now to a related argument that connects people with place, and suggests that living in a place, and having relationships and projects in a place, can give rise to an entitlement to exercise *jurisdiction* by a group in the place. In this section, I consider arguments about the way in which we interact with resources through creating rules that govern us; how or under what conditions they can be acquired, transferred, and how they can be used. In some respects, this argument about jurisdictional authority applies to both generic resources (which by definition are almost always located within a particular territory) and specific resources, and I will, in the next section, consider how a political community ought to frame their conventional rules and laws to consider both kinds of claims.

Some of the most contested issues around resources concerns which collective group ought to be in control of what resources and what level of authority ought to exercise jurisdiction over them. There are two dominant views: the cosmopolitan view that natural resources should be controlled by everyone equally or humanity at large, which suggests some kind of global government; and the opposite view, which is the current international law position, according to which resources are part of the state's territorial right, and that states have, and ought to have, 'permanent sovereignty' over resources falling within their jurisdiction. This doctrine was mainly pressed by developing countries as a form of leverage over richer countries who, they feared, were likely to try to gain control over the weaker party's resources, but is often asserted by states to justify their control in the international context.

The fundamental presupposition of the view that political communities should have jurisdictional authority over natural resources is that we are not isolated or atomistic individuals: we have collective identities, and projects that involve relationships with other people in a place; in fact, we define ourselves in a moral landscape made up primarily of a matrix of relationships with others – obligations, entitlements and dilemmas that we face not only as individuals but as members of groups. Unlike single-interest or voluntary groups, these are encompassing groups that share a collective identity that is rooted in geographical space, and in symbiotic relations with the land and resources within the area that the group lives in. Think here of indigenous people who require a dense rainforest to live their way of life, which may involve hunting and fishing and a semi-nomadic existence. Fishing communities or farming communities depend on access to resources but also are integrally related to social relations that are valuable in themselves. In that case we might say that these are dependent on certain relations of production, but that they encompass the entire way of life of the community: they shape communal practices, such as what people eat, what kind of homes they live in, and the family relations that they consider important. In the case of such rooted, encompassing communities, the members have a strong interest in collective control over resources.

It is not difficult to see the link between collective self-determination and control over resources. As I've argued elsewhere, jurisdictional authority over resources is an important dimension of collective self-determination.[9] If people lack control over the land that they live on, the water that they drink and swim in, then, to that extent, they lack robust forms of collective self-determination (though they might still have lesser forms of self-determination or be self-determining along other dimensions). Consider the Lakota Sioux, who have resisted strip mining in the Black Hills, because they regard the Hills as sacred. If they are to be self-determining, it is clear that they would need to have the power, the jurisdictional authority to make rules regarding the Black Hills. If they want the hills to remain untouched, because they regard them as sacred, they need to be able to exercise control over the Hills and to prevent the Hills from being destroyed through mining. This shows why it is fundamental to group self-determination that members of the group are able to make rules regarding important elements of their collective existence. Where people's lives are closely bound up with the land and resources where they live, they cannot exercise control if someone else or some other group can make decisions for this area. What they want is not simply access to a particular resource, nor to compensation for mining there (which in the case of the Lakota Sioux, they have refused) but the capacity to make rules that control the land, the water and the resources where they live. Similar arguments have been made by other groups: by the Sámi who have sacred sites in and around Inari in northern Finland, which they argue must be protected from development;[10] the Ogoni people who live in the Niger Delta and seek control over oil production that is polluting their water; and pastoralists who seek to prevent irrigation dams that alter the migratory patterns of the animals on which they depend.

The self-determination argument justifies control

over resources but not the current international law doctrine of permanent sovereignty over resources.[11] In fact, it denies both of the two main components of the permanent sovereignty position. First, it does not justify the state as the main holder of jurisdictional authority over resources but conceives of the fundamental holder of that authority as 'the people' (although of course the people's agency is typically exercised through institutions of the state). But the relevant 'people' may not correspond to all the people within the territorial domain of the state: there often are groups of people within a state who are in the right kind of encompassing relations with one another and with land and resources, where land is integral to their way of life, and they are the ones that should exercise jurisdictional authority locally over resources where they live. This is true of indigenous people, who are closely connected to the land and to resources, and also have a separate collective identity as a people in their own right (though they do not seek a state of their own, often because they lack capacity – they are too small and/or marginalized to effectively discharge state functions).

Second, this argument does not justify the claim that sovereign authority over resources is or ought to be 'permanent'. Indeed, I can think of no theorist who argues for this position, in part because the justificatory argument for such control operates only in certain cases, under specific conditions, and we can imagine that over time these conditions may not obtain. For example, suppose an indigenous group lives in the Amazon and pursues a way of life there that is integrally connected to the river basin and the rainforest and they therefore argue that they should have collective authority over these resources. I think they could mount a good argument for why they ought to be the group that has authority over resources there, either exclusively or with other relevant groups. However, it would be difficult to argue for their *permanent* sovereignty, since their relationship to the resource may change: the group may cease to be a relevant identity-conferring group; the members may after a time not be mobilized to exercise any form of collective self-determination over their lives; and they may cease to relate to the land in a way that would justify rights of control over it.

Conclusion

The central arguments examined herein make claims to particular resources, to particular areas of the natural world, and suggest that it is reasonable for these claims to be met. They are often based on an individual's or group's relationship with the place and their centrality in the life-plans, goals and aspirations of particular individuals and groups.

A secondary, and in part defensive, sub-theme of this chapter is that once the precise arguments are examined carefully – whether they are individual or collective, what exactly is being claimed and who holds the duty – the apparent counter-examples (e.g., the fox-hunting, mansion-loving aristocrat) that purport to discredit this form of argument are revealed as not on target.

4

Resource Conflict

The story told in the previous chapters – about the importance of attachment to land and the various different ways that we are related to it – seems plausible and attractive, but it raises two serious objections, which must now be addressed. The first is a general criticism to the effect that the pluralist theory of entitlement to resources that I've offered is insufficient because there is bound to be conflict among rival claims, and so needs to be supplemented with a principle for resolving such conflicts and/or prioritizing different claims. The second comes from a cosmopolitan direction, and raises the challenge that, while attachment and self-determination may be important values, resources should be subject to some kind of tax and transfer system, in the name of global equality.

Resource Conflict

An important challenge to my pluralist theory of entitlement to resources is the possibility of conflict among rival claims. I have discussed (1) basic rights, which is a principle of entitlement to resources based on the fact that humans need them, as a matter of survival, and is based on our (humans') relationship of *consumption* with the natural world; (2) desert, which I've understood primarily as a second-order claim to desert under justified rules, which I've theorized primarily in terms of relations of *production*; (3) *legitimate expectations* and other kinds of *historical* claims to resources; (4) *jurisdictional authority* and claims to control resources; and (5) a *stewardship* relationship, to preserve some resources for future generations. I will argue for this last relationship in the chapter that follows. Clearly, these various claims can conflict. Private property, especially private ownership of the means of production, can conflict with basic rights. The propertyless may be unable to secure the basic conditions of subsistence and security that I argued was necessary in chapter 2. Legitimate expectations can conflict with trusteeship relations – for example, if people have come to rely on greenhouse gas-emitting technology, which jeopardizes the climate and puts many (present and future) people's lives in danger. Basic rights can conflict with both legitimate expectations and jurisdictional authority claims, as when the urban poor demand the benefits of developing the resources of the rainforest, to address their poverty, and this may be opposed by indigenous people, whose way of life in the Amazonian jungle may be incompatible with this development. And these are just the conflicts that may arise among claimants living at the same time. If we satisfy the needs of everyone now, but do that through using up non-renewable resources, are we guilty of contributing to an intergenerational injustice? More specifically, as a matter of justice, what level and/or kind of resources must we bequeath to future generations?

One solution to the problem of resource conflict is to reduce all claims to a common metric, such as equality of welfare or equality of opportunities for welfare. Another approach is foundational, such as is evinced by a collective ownership theory. I agree with respect to the latter that needs are important, and can constrain the entitlements that I've outlined above – for example, to collective self-determination or to meeting legitimate expectations – but I've also criticized a monistic approach to the natural world, as insensitive to the diversity of ways in which we, individually and collectively, interact with the goods on our Earth and the value attendant on these ways. It's also not clear how exactly one can generate a value-neutral or culturally neutral metric to deal with these various cases.[1] If one group values a natural thing in one way and another group in another way, why is appealing to need the trumping consideration? And what does this theory advocate when one or more individuals or groups both claim that they need a particular physical thing (albeit for different reasons and in ways that are mutually incompatible)? The usual move in response to those claims is that one group gets to compensate the other but this raises as many questions as it resolves, because it could be that one group views the resource in a way that would permit compensation whereas the second has a more intrinsic relationship to that resource.

In this chapter, I adopt a version of the approach to resource conflict pioneered by Waldron in relation to rights conflicts, where he suggests that the most appropriate way to evaluate what is at stake in any conflict is by considering the answers to the following questions, which I've adapted for my purposes below.[2] What values are at stake in any conflict? What is the relationship of the resource to the value? How direct is the relation? Is there a way to realize some aspect of the value pointed to by each of the claimants (even if this doesn't realize the value to the maximum extent)? This last question is procedurally important, since it confers respect on each of the claimants, and tries to search for ways in which we don't have unmitigated conflict. And what are the long-term and more general effects of certain kinds of resource use? Since we are dealing with humans' relations to the planet, this necessarily brings in our obligations to non-humans, who might rely on the existence of certain ecosystems, and also bears on our obligations to future generations.

Using this more complicated and contextual set of questions provides a more accurate picture of what is normatively at stake than the sole focus on needs to determine our rights and obligations. Although it is true that people need food and water and other things to live, and that this gives rise to a moral right to the necessities of life, it doesn't follow that needs-based claims should get priority all the way down in any particular case of resource conflict. This point is made by Waldron in a compelling discussion of the merits of triage, which is often used in hospitals to assess the rival claims of various patients, who all in one sense have a right to health care. Waldron points out that the triage nurse (in his example) considers all the people who come to the emergency room. Clearly some people's needs are more urgent and more serious than others. But while the most urgent and serious cases should be dealt with first, it doesn't follow that the relation is one of lexical priority, by which I mean that the most important value (life) necessarily trumps other values, such as being free of pain or having a good quality of life, all the way down. If I am in the emergency room, in pain, with a broken arm, then a more urgent case – a traffic accident victim – should, obviously, be treated first, and treated until the point when it is safe for the doctor to leave the person in the charge of someone else and move on to different patients. But the broken arm patient shouldn't have to wait until the more urgent case or the more serious case is restored to full health. It's not just that that might take days. It's also that the broken arm patient has claims too, and her claims should be met as soon as there are resources available to be diverted to her needs, even if her claim has to wait until the most urgent case has to be dealt with *to some extent.* This example shows that need is very important but other claims have to be kept in view, and dealt with to the extent possible, so that potential conflict is mitigated.

Let's adapt Waldron's approach to cases of

resource conflict. We can incorporate Waldron's insights about relative value not having trumping force, keeping the various claimants and different values in view, and assessing how direct the claim is to realizing the said value and especially considering whether the claim could be met by access to a generic resource.

One kind of conflict is between various individuals wanting to claim the same resource. Intra-resource conflicts are often not philosophically interesting, since the rules around property – acquisition, transfer and so on – are especially useful in dealing with this form of conflict. But it's worth noting that not all forms of resource consumption are equally likely to generate conflict. We should distinguish between those pursuits that involve the *non-subtractive* use of resources, and those pursuits that *deplete* resources so that conferring the resource on one person means that that resource is unavailable for others. An eco-hiking trip in the rainforest, to spot orangutans or rare birds, and enjoy its wonderful biodiversity, is an example of a non-subtractive use. This form of interaction has to be strictly regulated, of course: the hikers may have to be confined to particular paths or to canopy walks because, otherwise, they will disturb the very animal and plant life that makes the place special in the first place. Also, to the extent that people seek to be tourists in remote places and do not want those places to be crowded with throngs of other tourists, the rate of access to these places may need to be limited. However, if this regulation is done properly, the fact that person 'X' hiked in the rainforest does not mean that other people cannot hike there. Although there may be competition to enjoy a resource, in the sense that access to the rainforest may turn out to be a scarce good, it is not a *resource conflict* in the ordinary way.

Waldron's second and third questions – concerning the values at stake and the relationship of the value to the thing in question – direct us to consider whether the person's or community's relationship to the resource is one where substitution is possible (e.g., where I need water but not access to your particular river) or whether the value can only be realized through access and control over a specific resource or set of resources (where substitution is not possible). This distinction is relevant not only to an all-things-considered judgement, but also to the way we try to mitigate conflict. Need-based claims generally can be met by ensuring that the person has access to resources *in general*, but does not require access to *particular* resources. People need a sufficient quantity of food and water, access to adequate shelter and so on, but they don't need access to a particular water body or particular home. In other cases, the claim is highly particularized: this is true of the example of a particular community's way of life, which is intimately bound up with the flora and fauna of the rainforest. The indigenous person in the rainforest, for example, has a deep knowledge of its contours, where to find animals, where to fish and so on; and the claim to be entitled to live there, in that geographical space, cannot normally be replaced by living somewhere else. This isn't meant to imply that one type of claim is stronger than another, but it does mean that a claim to a general good is more flexible than claims to particular goods when there is competition between two claims to the same resource; and this fact is relevant to any attempt to mitigate conflicts among resources.

Let us turn now to particular cases where the principles that I've endorsed in chapters 2 and 3 could conflict with each other. Private property has the obvious *potential* to interfere with the basic subsistence rights of others, and specifically non-appropriators, but it's not a *necessary* conflict. It would be a necessary conflict if I thought of property rights as a natural moral right, which is an extension of our liberty rights. However, I adopt the more conventional view that property rights – the rules of acquisition, transfer, exchange and so on – are created by the state or jurisdictional authority, and justified because they help to meet social goods. The usual liberal justification is that private property helps to increase the overall wealth of the society, so that even the worst off are better off than they would be under rules that enforced equality.[3] But I've accepted a pluralist account of the values that should be endorsed, which includes subsistence rights. Thus, the rules of property can and should include redistributive taxation, constraints on monopolies, restrictions on inheritance and other kinds of limits on private property acquisition consistent with meeting the basic rights of others. The scope of a legitimate property right can be conceived in a way that prevents an unavoidable conflict between private ownership and basic needs. I also argued that self-determination is consistent with taxing the benefit that derives from use of resources, as long as the collectively self-determining community or communities make decisions to control the resources in question.[4]

It would be a mistake, though, to think that the rules in question can always be specified in ways that will reduce conflict among the different claimants and types of claims. Some resource conflicts are unavoidable. Consider the case where an individual or community of people have come to rely on a particular technology, and it is later discovered that various kinds of harms to future people are predictably linked to this technology. As in the case of triage, the claim of the person who unknowingly came to depend on the particular technology or resource does not disappear from view. Although we have to move to a situation which is more just, we must do so in a way that treats fairly the claims and interests of people who unknowingly came to rely on this harmful technology. I suggested earlier, in the discussion of the students who prepare for university through A levels or International Baccalaureate schools, the possibility of a grandfathering principle or some kind of time-adjustment for the person to adapt to the new situation and/or compensation for his or her reliance. In this way, as in the example of triage, the claims of all have to be kept in view, to reduce the possibility of unmitigated conflict.

Basic Rights to Subsistence and the Cosmopolitan Challenge

It may be obvious from the foregoing how exactly this approach will deal with the cosmopolitan challenge outlined at the beginning of this chapter, which points out that, if a state or political community exercises jurisdiction over a geographical area, controlling resources there, then this might mean that the resources are unavailable to people in other parts of the world, who find that they are excluded from them. This looks problematic: resource-rich political communities would then be able to hog the resources for themselves, excluding the global poor from accessing those resources and benefitting from them.

It is important to see, though, precisely what is problematic about this. I've argued that people are very differently related to land and to the natural world: they have different relations as producers, as self-determining communities, and as individuals. I am denying therefore that there is an automatic presumption of *equality*. It is hard to see why people should have an equal substantial entitlement when they are very differently related to the natural world and to the places in it. However, everyone needs some resources – clean air to breathe, clean water to drink, food, shelter and so on. This was recognized by the theorists who talked about common ownership of the world, but can be understood more directly in Shue's language of basic rights (to subsistence). In that dimension (of need), everyone has equal rights. We all are physical beings, who have basic rights to subsistence, and some space on Earth. Each person is entitled to that, and the argument advanced here recognizes this equal entitlement.

In the previous chapter I argued that control over resources is implicit in the value of self-determination. The idea developed there was that people living on the land, who are co-creating rules of justice and exercising control over the collective conditions of their lives, should be able to make choices about how the land and other natural goods where they live are used. They should be able to make decisions about such things as whether it should be held individually or collectively, whether some parts of it should be protected wetlands or left unused on the grounds of religious or cultural significance, for example. If people do not have this capacity, they cannot exercise any serious form of collective self-determination. They would then be unable to make key decisions about the way in which their communities and their collective lives were organized around the natural world, and would be unable to express their own values vis-à-vis the physical world that they live in. However, it does not follow from this justification that the flow of money that is generated from natural resources and the economy in general can't be subject to redistribution in order to meet others' basic subsistence rights. The argument that I developed, then, to realize the value of self-determination, is an argument about jurisdictional *control*, but does not automatically confer a right to the stream of benefit that may flow from that control. It is therefore consistent with taxation in order to meet the basic rights of people in the world.

On my argument, then, the entitlement of everyone to basic rights of subsistence and security is a limitation on the exercise of collective self-determination (and other related entitlements). By this I mean that these claims are legitimate only if they are consistent with these basic rights. The term 'consistent with' can be used in a number of different ways, some more stringent than others. In my use, the term 'consistent with' does not mean that the basic rights of everyone must already be met, but rather the weaker claims that (a) political communities in which people are collectively self-determining, and in which people create rules to organize their collective lives, are themselves necessary for people to secure their basic rights; (b) the subsistence rights of others can be met without violating collective self-determination; and (c) collective self-determination is not the reason why these rights aren't met. Fairer global rules regarding trade and development, as well as substantial redistribution from the wealthy to the poorer parts of the world would be sufficient to meet subsistence rights globally.[5] Moreover, as the first two points above indicate, the rules surrounding property and resource rights are not only important for people to achieve control over their existence, but are an important element in the solution to the 'tragedy of the commons', and creating an environment in which people can escape deprivation.

Does this mean that political communities have obligations of justice to exploit resources when doing so could help meet the basic needs of the global poor? The general picture behind this question is that, in order to be collectively self-determining in an effective way, groups have entitlement to set the terms under which natural resources are used in the first place, and they decide not to use a particular resource. If the basic needs of people outside the state or outside the self-determining political community can be met only if states give up some control over their 'resources', are they required to do so? Is it so important for these groups to maintain their way of life and not cultivate a resource that they should be permitted to do so even if this meant that the basic needs of everyone could not be met? This is an important challenge to the framework that I've offered because in that scenario it does seem that not cultivating resources to the fullest operates rather like an expensive taste that justice should not countenance fulfilling. This would be a problem for my theory because I've argued that there are significant normative relationships at stake here, and that control over resources is necessary to meaningful self-determination, which in itself is of significant moral value.

I think there is a theoretical possibility that failure to exploit potential resources (resources in the eyes of some) may jeopardize subsistence rights. But I do not think, for the reasons set out above, that this means that subsistence rights should automatically trump the right to collective self-determination, simply because subsistence is morally more important than self-determination. The obvious reason for this is that there are multiple possibilities for meeting subsistence rights and different communities could do so in different ways. In any case of conflict, it is important that we examine how direct the relationship is between the fundamental interest in question (the interest that the right is supposed to protect) and the policy. Here, I can only express scepticism that mining the various minerals in the Black Hills or drilling oil in the ecologically fragile High Arctic is directly necessary to meet subsistence rights, and that there are no other alternatives.

Of course, one can imagine cases where access to a particular natural resource – which is rare, found in only one place and necessary to cure a terminal illness – is indeed necessary to meet subsistence rights. And in that case, the people who live in the place have an interest in collective self-determination, which gives them a presumptive right to make decisions about the natural world in which they live. In this case, the interest in self-determination over the resource is outweighed by the interests of people who are dying from a preventable disease. In general, then, we need to weigh exactly how necessary the resource is to the prevention or treatment of the disease (is it the only cure?) and whether the interest in collective self-determination absolutely requires the non-exploitation (of the resource) decision, which, where land is viewed as sacred, might be the case, or whether the community's central preferences and interests can be addressed consistent with exploitation of its resources.

Conclusion

In this chapter, I've argued that, while needs are the most pressing and important claim, it doesn't follow that a needs-based claim will necessarily trump other sorts of claims because the relationship of that value (addressing needs) to the resource may not be direct: it may be probabilistic; the need could be met in other ways; and so on. I've argued for a contextual approach to addressing resource conflict that recognizes the weightiness of the claims, the question of who has the duty; and the fact that the claimant could be an individual or a community and that these might conflict. This addresses the two criticisms that I think arise most naturally from a pluralist account of resource justice – that there has to be some limits on expectation-type arguments or self-determination arguments and that we need a way to address direct resource conflicts.

The argument of this chapter is insufficient in one respect: it is confined to conflicts among presently existing individuals and communities, and sets aside the claims of future generations. Yet that could be conceived of as a case of resource conflict too, between the claims of people living now, who make decisions about resources and exercise self-determination through their political communities, and the resource claims of future people. If we satisfy the needs of everyone now, but do that through using up non-renewable resources, are we guilty of contributing to an intergenerational injustice? It is to this question that we now turn.

5

Future Generations
and Resource Justice

In chapter 3, I argued that individual human beings have basic rights to subsistence and security, which includes access to food, clean water, shelter, clean air and other resources related to those two rights. That discussion, focused mainly on the subsistence needs of individual persons, was insufficient, however. A needs-based account of course must consider the immediate survival of particular existing individuals, but should also include the medium- and long-term survival of persons, including persons yet born. More specifically, as a matter of justice, what level and/or kind of resources do we owe to future generations? As before, resources are to be understood broadly to include not only individualized resources, such as gold or oil or land, but also such things as the carbon-sequestering capacity of the atmosphere, the oceans and the Earth's rainforests.

The principle that is most often invoked in discussions of intergenerational justice and resources is that of sustainability. This is a natural principle for any theory that takes seriously the claims of future generations. It assumes that we need to consider our relation to the world, not just along the dimensions of production and consumption, and the other claims discussed above, but also in terms of our relationship to the natural world as stewards of the planet for future generations of humans (and, arguably, other animals).

What do we mean by 'sustainability'? This principle implies that we have obligations to preserve the very conditions for making life worth living (or liveable at all) in the future – although there are of course disagreements about how much we ought to do to preserve this, and disagreement about what exactly should be sustained.[1] Since we all rely on this blue planet, we need to ensure that it is liveable for the next generation, and we have a duty to protect and take responsibility for it. The problem with the idea of sustainability, however, is that it cannot be explicated without relying on a deeper theory of what ought to be sustained. The way that this is ordinarily approached in the political theory literature is entirely in terms of principles to govern a basket of resources, broadly conceived – asking what we are required, permitted or prohibited from doing with respect to that basket of goods. The possibilities are: savings, dissavings and status quo, where savings means that we transfer more (of the basket of goods or resources) than we inherited; dissavings means that we pass on less to future generations; and status quo means that we pass on the same amount.

This raises the question: *what* is it that we, the current generation, might save or dissave or keep at the status quo? As noted above, this depends on what the theorist thinks matters. The concept of sustainability, which is often thought to be at the heart of theories of intergenerational justice, is parasitic on the larger theory of what matters: for rights theorists, it will be the preservation of rights (human rights, basic rights); for welfare utilitarians, it will be conditions for welfare or preference satisfaction, however that is defined; for equality of opportunity theorists, it will be equal opportunity sets. Appealing to sustainability doesn't change that logic, because the ideal of sustainability expresses the intuition that we should not short-change our successors, but if that means that we should not leave them with less of what matters, then the content of sustainability will depend crucially on what we think matters.[2]

It also implies that the resources in the basket are potentially substitutable. This point is made by Brian Barry in relation to welfare satisfaction (in an example that illustrates the problematic nature of this assumption): if what matters is equal opportunities for want-satisfaction, and if plastic trees are as satisfying as real ones, there is no reason to worry about the destruction of the world's trees as long as resources exist to manufacture plastic replacements in sufficient numbers.[3] In this chapter, I try to fill in what this largely formal notion of sustainability might mean with reference to natural resources, and identify particular places and key ecosystems as central to ensuring that a healthy and liveable Earth is passed on to future generations. It rejects the assumption that resources should be thought of as an (essentially substitutable) bundle.

The core idea of sustainability, then, is that each generation should try to sustain enough of what matters to pass on to the next generation. That is easy enough when we have extra goods, but what about when the basic rights of present and future people conflict? If some people's basic rights (to subsistence and security) are not met in the present, can we use additional resources now to meet those needs, even if this reduces the level of resources of future generations? The answer is yes, for various reasons: the rights of people living now are more urgent than those of future people. We also have more confidence about how our actions affect the basic rights of the present generation, and even more confidence about the needs of people who live now (as compared to hypothetical future people). For this reason, it seems reasonable to permit dis-savings now, for the sake of the basic rights of currently existing people. Yet in many cases this (basic rights now versus basic rights in the future) is a false conflict: usually the reason why basic rights are not met has to do with inequality and institutional inefficiencies, and these problems can be addressed without sacrificing the future.

There is, however, an exception to this prioritiz-ing of the current generation's basic rights: there are some vital areas of our planet which must be kept in a healthy state, and not to do so involves a wrongful imposition of risk. Although we have stewardship obligations everywhere on the planet, not all places are equally important when it comes to preserving the basic conditions for acceptable life in the future. The central argument of this chapter is that considerations of intergenerational justice prohibit us from threatening the sustainability of key resource areas that are vital to the health of future generations – the oceans and water resources generally, the polar regions, rainforests, the atmosphere (which impacts on the polar regions and the oceans). These must be preserved in a healthy state to ensure that we do not impose a serious and wrongful risk of harm on future generations.

To make that argument persuasive, however, I need to show why we should have more stringent obligations with respect to some places than others. This requires us to reject the usual assumption in the future generation literature – that is, the very idea of a 'basket of goods' that we should transfer to the next generation. The usual description of the basic grammar of intergenerational justice,[4] in terms of three categories (savings, dissavings and status quo) across three modalities (prohibition, permission and obligation) does not tell us anything about the basket of goods that we ought to transfer to the next generation. Yet, that is a very important question for people interested in resource justice. I argue that the metaphor of a single 'basket' of goods does not sufficiently recognize that some natural places have a more important relationship to the health of our planet than others. To live in a sustainable world, we need to preserve carbon sinks, key water resources and biodiversity hotspots, which are important for regulating the planet's overall climate. Some elements of the alleged basket cannot be substituted by other goods, but are necessary to the long-term future of human and animal species, indeed the planet as a whole.[5]

There are two arguments for this non-substitutability claim: the first one bears on the fact that some of these places are unoccupied, so some of the competitive uses that we normally think might be at work do not apply. This argument is directed at rights to resource exploitation in these areas. The second argument has interconnected empirical and normative parts, and has more radical constraining implications. The main concept that I develop in this chapter is that jeopardizing the health of these places involves the *wrongful imposition of risk* on future generations.

Resource Extraction and Stewardship

The first argument – which is about resource extraction in places that are either not occupied, or, sometimes (as with the rainforests), only thinly occupied – lays stress on two facts: first, that our relationship to these places is different than places where we live, and where we therefore have to make choices that involve balancing a number of different considerations; and, second, that many of these places (oceans, rainforests, the polar regions) are vitally important to the health of the planet. In the cases of the oceans, the seabed and large areas of both polar regions, we do not interact with these places as producers or consumers, nor do we have place-related plans with respect to them. They are not obviously connected to the territorial rights of any particular community. I argued earlier that people are entitled to exercise jurisdictional authority over the place where they live, and the land and resources that are contained in that physical space, because this was necessary to their collective self-determination. But this doesn't apply to these places. Although countries may claim jurisdictional authority, it is hard to see what would ground this, other than the need to protect these places from general predation, which is consistent with the sustainability principle advanced here.

Since these places (or at least some parts of these places, in the case of the Arctic) are not central to the lives of particular people on Earth nor the collective self-determination of particular communities, some of the usual arguments that compete with the environmental ones do not apply. We often think that there is a general liberty right to extract resources in land that is empty, which relies on the idea that unclaimed or un-owned land is not valuable to anyone, but, by transforming it into something of use, it contributes to increasing the 'general stock' of wealth available to humankind, in Locke's memorable phrase. This was generally accepted in much liberal political theory in the past, and does seem to embody a number of widely accepted assumptions about human liberty, human needs and the rights of people to satisfy their needs and the positive transformative effects of human labour.[6] On this view, which was of course central to justifying both settler colonialism and the imperial order that followed, un-owned or unclaimed land or resources should be 'up for grabs'.

Now, however, we should reject this picture of relatively unimpeded access to unused resources on unoccupied land to create property rights. Because no political community can make a special claim to the land and resources in an unoccupied area, the argument relies on the questionable empirical assumption that we can correlate resource extraction with general benefit. This assumption was generally held when this view was hegemonic from the seventeenth century until very recently, but we now have a richer scientific understanding of the inter-relationship between resource development, especially where this involves transformative extraction activities, and the common good of all humanity. There is now overwhelming evidence that resource extraction poses a serious threat in the fragile and quite specialized ecosystems that we are considering – the polar regions, the ocean, the seabed, rainforests.[7]

Some might argue that a complete prohibition on resource extraction in these unoccupied but very important (to the planet) places is unwarranted. There may be resource extraction that can be done without serious ecological damage. Indeed, it might be claimed that harvesting such resources would help offset the cost of ecological clean-up, a point that I will consider below. I think this is true with respect to fishing the oceans, or controlled logging, which can be done in a regulated way, or palm oil plantations that are on already existing farmland, and do not involve the destruction of rainforests, but not resource extraction activities in other unoccupied areas.

I cannot of course preclude the possibility of an environmentally safe form of resource extraction, or a technological fix for the current destructive levels of greenhouse gases in the atmosphere, but I think a precautionary principle is in order, because of the fragility of these areas and their importance to the health of the planet and the people living on it.

What do I mean by a precautionary principle? One of the first references to a precautionary principle was in the United Nation's Rio Declaration of 1992, which emphasized the problem with high-risk, complex processes that are not completely understood, and decision making under uncertainty.[8] When faced with potentially catastrophic risks, the thought is that we can't always know in advance what the probabilities of risk are, or indeed what the risks are, since the processes themselves are not fully understood and we should therefore err on the side of caution. This isn't a proper *principle*, but it does suggest that a cost–benefit analysis is inappropriate in conditions where we are operating under such uncertainty and the magnitude of potential harm is high. A red line rule about resource extraction is further justified by the possible consequences of a more nuanced rule involving the exercise of judgement in this matter: states, which would be in a position to tax the resource wealth so created, have an incentive to use that discretion to adopt a permissive stance.

Stewardship and the Substitutability of Resources Assumption

It might be objected that the argument advanced above would be persuasive if the only thing that we needed to do with respect to resources is not extract them. It suggests that the main cost is an opportunity cost, related to a ban on resource extraction activities. But this is not an accurate picture: stewardship is a much more expensive proposition, as is clear in the argument I develop below, against the substitutability of all 'resources'. This argument proceeds in two parts – empirical and then normative.

The empirical argument is connected to strong scientific evidence of the importance of key areas of the planet – the oceans, the atmosphere, the polar regions and the rainforests – for important climactic processes on Earth. Obviously, the fish stocks in the ocean are depleted and some species are in danger because of over-fishing. More seriously, many parts of the ocean are effectively dead, and this dead zone is increasing, due to increased pollution and increased calcification, related to over-production of carbon dioxide.[9] Large areas of the ocean are also now being used as a dumping ground for plastics, which are toxic.[10] Rainforests are similarly vital for the health of the planet, for two important reasons: they are an important source of biodiversity, which itself is intrinsically and consequentially valuable (although in the latter case, sometimes for reasons that we can't yet predict); and they play an important role sequestering large amounts of carbon. The polar regions, too, are ecologically fragile, which makes resource exploitation extremely dangerous, and they are also vulnerable to climate change. Indeed, one of the biggest fears expressed by climate scientists concerns the thawing of the Arctic permafrost which itself harbours large amounts of carbon, which would be released into the atmosphere if it melts, and would seriously affect climactic processes here on Earth.[11] Thus, any serious consideration of the health of the oceans and the North and South Poles has to take into account the effect of excess greenhouse gases on these places, which, I argue below, necessitates serious restrictions on that resource (the resource being the carbon-sequestering capacity of the atmosphere, the rainforests and the oceans).

The second, normative point, which follows from the empirical evidence about the importance of these places, is that the destruction of these places can't be conceived in the same way as other resources, where losses of one resource could be offset or compensated for by gains in other areas.

On the contrary, it represents a wrongful form of risk imposition for future generations. What do I mean by wrongful imposition of risk? Obviously, harming people now is wrong. Imposing a risk of harm may also be wrong.[12] In the course of making decisions over our lives we do impose risks on other people. Indeed, almost every action that we take imposes some risk on other people, so that a total ban on risk imposition is not plausible.[13]

In his work on risk imposition, Sven Ove Hansson has argued that risk imposition may be acceptable if it's reciprocal, and he specifies that this means that the exposure to risk is '*either* outweighed by a greater benefit for that person herself, *or* part of a social practice in which other persons are exposed to the same risk'. He also specifies that the benefits to the person or persons from this practice should outweigh the risk; and all the parties to the social practice ought to exercise some control over the rules of the practice in question.[14] This account recognizes the importance of individual rights and of making mutually beneficial adjustments, but also prohibits potentially exploitative arrangements in which some persons, or set of persons, are exposed to risk in order to achieve benefits for others. If these conditions don't obtain, risk imposition can be described as wrongful.

In the case of the destruction of rainforests, the oceans and the excessive production of greenhouse gases, all the conditions for wrongful risk imposition apply. Carbon emissions are intentional: we have known about the risks of human-induced climate change and potential harms resulting from carbon pollution at least since 1990, when the first Intergovernmental Panel on Climate Change (IPCC) report was issued, so we can no longer say that agents are excusably ignorant of the consequences of their actions.[15] There may be disagreements about the precise models, timelines and tipping points, but there is a scientific consensus on the relationship between this activity and harm. There is also no possibility of reciprocity or mutuality because time is one-directional and our actions can be conceived, at best, as disregarding the interests of future generations in favour of patterns of production and consumption that benefit us (or some of us) now. And the potential harm is grave, contributing to the premature death and rights-deficits of many millions of future people. The conditions for wrongful imposition are met by the destruction of rainforests, pollution of oceans, pollution of the atmosphere and the consequent destruction of the environment of the polar regions and the health of the planet. There is the intentional imposition of risk on someone else, presumably for expected gain to oneself (because these forms of pollution and actions that reduce or eliminate various forms of biodiversity are connected to increased production, increased consumption of goods).

On my account, sustainability is not primarily about preserving a certain level or basket of resources, but requires also the preservation of these key resources for future generations. Given our scientific knowledge of these interconnected processes on the health of the planet, we should regard the destruction of these areas as an instance of the wrongful imposition of risk on future generations of people. The only exception to this is a dystopian scenario, very far from where we are at present, which is that the only reason to wrongfully impose these risks on others is because not doing so wrongfully imposes risks on the existence of people now. And to make good that argument it would need to be the case that there was no other way to meet the basic needs of present people.

Central to the argument of this chapter is the thought that some goods or some resources can't be exchanged for others. Social, economic or cultural goods ought not to be exchanged for some natural goods and some natural goods should be regarded as not substitutable for goods of other kinds. Loss of the rainforest and a living ocean – both of which have unique features in terms of the ecosystem/ biodiversity that they harbour – cannot be compensated for by increased goods of another kind; and this point should be incorporated into our account of sustainability, which is at the heart of our conception of intergenerational justice. In the case of a direct and unavoidable conflict between the most serious basic rights of people living now and similar rights of future people, the claims of people currently alive ought to have priority. But if we are in this situation, and the very survival of currently existing humans is at stake, then it follows also that the very survival of future people is also at stake. This is not the scenario that we are in now, or anything close to it, but we are now jeopardizing the basic rights of future people through the destruction of these areas.

Who Ought to be the Steward?

Once we accept that the primary relationship of people to the oceans, the rainforests, the polar regions and so on is not that of ownership and/or resource extraction but that of stewardship in the interests of common humanity, there is the question of who or what institution ought to discharge that duty, and how the costs should be paid for. Since the idea of stewardship involves protection and maintenance of the area for the common good of humanity, it might seem that the appropriate locus of jurisdiction – for the regulation or maintenance of the area in question – ought to fall to an international organization with coercive powers, charged with this responsibility.

Although we do have some international agencies in place, and these could be further strengthened and made more inclusive, the central problem is that there is not now, nor in the foreseeable future, an overarching organization with jurisdiction and enforcement capabilities over oceans or the Arctic or Earth's rainforests that could exercise a stewardship role effectively. The problem here is not a theoretical one, but a practical one. It is that there's no point in assigning an authority to carry out this function unless this is practically feasible. There are two senses of 'feasible': the binary sense, which is connected to logical consistency; and a scalar sense, in which feasibility refers to a measure of probability – how likely it is for something to happen or be agreed upon or implemented. The establishment of a multi-lateral agency with jurisdictional authority and coercive power over unoccupied resources is feasible in the first sense but not obviously in the second. Moreover, the organizations that we have now and in the foreseeable future are inadequate in two ways: they are only authoritative for those parties that agree to them, and, even then, the enforcement mechanisms are quite weak.

It's unlikely that we can get agreement on such an organization or conferring significant powers on existing transnational or international agencies in the comprehensive way that is needed in the foreseeable or even medium-term future. In the meantime, or instead (of that ideal), we could also imagine giving the responsibility to protect some of these areas to the most proximate capable agent who is likely to discharge this duty, and on whom there is a consensus that they are the appropriate or legitimate state or self-determining entity in that geographic space. Proximity matters because in the case of an environmental disaster, it is important to get to the area in question quickly, to identify the problem, to address it and possibly stop or reverse what is happening. It is therefore strongly related to capacity, by which I mean the ability to discharge this function. Capacity is a necessary condition for being a territorial rights-holder: after all, what would be the point of conferring authority to act as a steward over territory if the

103

designated agent or institution could not fulfil that responsibility?

The proximity and capacity principles don't uniquely pick out a particular state as the one to discharge this duty with respect to Earth's rainforests or sensitive environmental areas of the Arctic. In some cases, however, there is convergence at the international level on a particular state having authority over a geographical area, and, even if this convergence is for weak normative reasons, it is both legally and morally relevant. As David Hume noted, in cases of disagreement over property, we need a political order and a system of rules to avoid conflict (or, as I am arguing, stewardship of areas that are important to the health of the planet) and this suggests that we should accept convergence when it occurs to assign a steward in these areas.[16]

This may seem a very conventional view: Canada has territorial rights over its portion of the Arctic, Russia over its portion and so on. Similarly, Ecuador has control over its portion of the rainforest, Costa Rica over its. Territorial states that are accepted political authorities in other unoccupied or environmentally sensitive areas are picked out, for conventional reasons, as holders of jurisdictional authority to exercise stewardship over these places. In fact, though, the argument advanced here is more radical than this, because stewardship implies a success condition: a country could fail to act effectively as a steward, and its territorial rights be brought into question. The conventional argument picks out the current state, or the conventionally accepted state, as the one that ought to be the steward when we have a number of possible contenders, but this authority is contingent on the state actually performing this function.[17]

In places where there is no conventional authority – the oceans, for example – we need an international organization and we are under an obligation to create one if it doesn't exist and to strengthen existing international laws and international treaties. This is challenging and, again, feasibility considerations may have to enter in: if we cannot create a coercive international agency that can set rules, we can proceed by treaties as long as the main purpose is to create an institutional structure that will help us discharge our obligations to future generations.

Who Pays the Cost?

In the discussion of resource extraction, it may have seemed that stewardship primarily involves simple non-extraction of resources and that the primary cost is opportunity cost. This is not so, however. Stewardship can be quite expensive. First, there are some costs attached to protecting an area from external predation. The steward has to be in a position to regulate the area and enforce these regulations. These should be accepted by the territorial state that has control over the area, which may benefit in prestige terms from having this additional territory. In addition, as Chris Armstrong has argued, stewardship may involve clean-up of environmentally damaged areas, such as restoring coral reefs to their former healthy state, or attempting to re-freeze the permafrost to prevent the release of huge amounts of carbon into the atmosphere.[18] Since this is in the common interests of all humanity, and created by global processes such as the overall quantity of CO_2 in the atmosphere, it follows that these costs should be borne by all, and a global fund set up to finance and administer the efforts. Like the creation of a global or regional agency to exercise jurisdiction over these areas, this is probably not likely in the foreseeable future. This doesn't mean, however, that this isn't the right normative approach to unoccupied areas that are crucial for the health, indeed survival, of the planet.

Conclusion

In this chapter I have argued that we have stewardship obligations everywhere on the planet. We live
on this Earth and should produce and consume,
and exercise self-determination in ways that are
consistent with passing on to future generations a
planet that is sufficiently healthy that it can meet
their basic rights. It could perhaps be argued that
what is needed, when there has been mismanage-
ment in the past, is more than just status quo: that
what is needed is savings (that we need to pass on
more to the next generation, if the world is below
the appropriate threshold of sustainability so that
we can achieve the basic rights threshold). I accept
this with respect to the areas that the scientists
identify as important, as long as it doesn't jeopardize basic rights in the present. This may indeed be
necessary, if we think of ourselves as stewards,
which I will get to below.

Some may object that this view is not sufficiently
environmentally conscious. There are many places
on Earth of unique beauty – the rugged Canadian
Shield along Georgian Bay; the terraced rice pad-
dies of the Mù Cang Ch'ai region of Vietnam; the
Lake District of England. In all these places, there
are stewardship obligations. But in most places, we

engage in everyday human activities of production, consumption, self-determination and fulfilling our place-related plans, and these involve a variety of different normatively significant relations with the natural world. In this context, the interests of future people must compete with other sorts of claims of people living there now for use of resources. Because this is so, there will be various sorts of risks to the natural environment, and competing claims, which have to be balanced in the way described earlier. However, I've also argued that the scientific evidence about the interlocking nature of climate processes on Earth and a number of specific areas means that, in certain places that are key to sustaining the basic rights of people on Earth, the imperatives of sustainability are decisive.

6

Concluding Remarks

This book has argued that the way we interact with the natural world, how we use resources, share them, refrain from using them, and the terms under which we exercise control over them are crucially important issues for justice in our time and for future generations.

Human history has been marked by conflict over resources and this remains true today. In part, this is because we do not have a clear idea of how we should think about our relation to the natural world, or how to resolve resource conflicts, either procedurally (through our institutions) or conceptually (by having a map of what kinds of claims are legitimate and what are not).

One of the central themes of this book is that natural resources are special – but they are special, I think, not for the usual reason (that they are undeserved and therefore ought to be subject to redistribution) but because they are sometimes non-substitutable. Individual persons and communities interact with resources in ways that go beyond seeking welfare improvements or using resources to produce more goods. On the usual views, which I reject, the loss of a natural good can be compensated for by other kinds of goods – human-made goods, stocks and shares, and so on – as long as those goods satisfy preferences, equalize opportunities and so on.

I have given reasons for thinking that humans are related to the resources on Earth in a number of different ways, some of which challenge this typical thinking. The natural world, I have suggested in this book, can enter into our life plans in significant ways. We – individually and in the collective groups that matter to us – have a history with particular places, or particular pieces of land. We often care especially about them, and have come to rely on them for our life and sustenance, and this itself may generate duties. In other works, I have referred to this as a 'place-related' interest, but I have mainly discussed it with reference to particular geographical areas, and particular pieces of land.[1] However, I believe that these important relationships between human beings and the natural world can also apply to other kinds of natural resources in the world.

The theme of non-substitutability is also central to the chapter on intergenerational justice, which is focused on rejecting the idea that we need only sustain a set of opportunities or preference satisfaction or welfare into the future. What we need to sustain, I argue, is the life-giving properties of this planet. In part, this is so that basic rights of future people can be met, although I also gave a reason why we need to be concerned about whole ecosystems and biodiversity apart from that. We don't know precisely what the losses are when the rare amphibian species of Kiribati are lost forever, when, as a result of global warming, it finally sinks into the Pacific Ocean. However, I also suggest that the destruction of these islands and all things in them represents a wrongful imposition of risk on future generations. This is still, I concede, a human-related interest, but that is partly because I don't know how to argue for intrinsic value, except to say that I have a strong intuition that something of grave value might be lost.

We have all, I think, imbibed the image of Earth taken from space: a small blue planet, hurtling on its elliptical orbit around the Sun. This image reinforces the questions of this book: how are we to live together and share this planet, and interact with the natural world contained on it? This is a pressing question, which is at the heart of both present and intergenerational justice. I hope this book makes a contribution to the way we think about this question.

Notes

Chapter 1

1 See Margaret Moore, 'Natural Resources, Territorial Right and Global Distributive Justice', *Political Theory*, 40/1 (2012), 84–107.

2 Avery Kolers, *Land, Conflict, and Justice* (Cambridge: Cambridge University Press, 2009).

3 For a great discussion of diverse types of resources, which emphasizes the relationship between people, institutional structures and resources, see Elinor Ostrom, *Governing the Commons* (Cambridge: Cambridge University Press, 1990), and Elinor Ostrom, 'How Types of Goods and Property Rights Jointly Affect Collective Action', *Journal of Theoretical Politics*, 15/3 (2003), 239–70.

4 John Christman, *The Myth of Property* (Oxford: Oxford University Press, 1994). The economists' distinction between private goods, collective goods and pure public goods is also not discussed here,

because it is interested in who pays for such goods, and explains why public goods are under-supplied in a market, but is not that relevant to normative analysis.

5 John Locke, 'The Second Treatise of Government: An Essay Concerning the True Original, Extent and End of Civil Government', in *Political Writings of John Locke*, ed. with an introduction by David Wootton (New York: Penguin, 1993 [1681]); and A. John Simmons, *The Lockean Theory of Rights* (Princeton, NJ: Princeton University Press, 1982).

6 Liam Murphy and Thomas Nagel, *The Myth of Ownership: Taxes and Justice* (Oxford: Oxford University Press, 2002).

7 Kiribati is a relatively isolated group of Pacific islands which are home to unique species, especially of amphibians, which live nowhere else on the planet.

Chapter 2

1 This concept of ownership is developed from Tony Honoré and discussed in chapter 1.

2 John Simmons has a typology that corresponds roughly to these various ideas of the commons. See Simmons, *The Lockean Theory of Rights*, p. 238.

3 This conception is embodied in G. A. Cohen's story of Able and Infirm, whereby both Able and Infirm are joint owners of external natural resources, and each has a claim-right that the other not use the resource without their consent, and neither is there-

fore at liberty to use the resources. G. A. Cohen, *Self-Ownership, Freedom and Equality* (Cambridge: Cambridge University Press, 1995), pp. 95–8.

4 This point is made by Nozick in a passage that seems directed against a free-for-all view of the commons. Robert Nozick, *Anarchy, State and Utopia* (New York: Basic Books, 1974), p. 175.

5 This point is made in David Miller, *National Responsibility and Global Justice* (Oxford: Oxford University Press, 2007), pp. 57–8.

6 Armstrong argues that, from the perspective of the individual person, natural resources are not any less or more undeserved than many other features of human life. This thought suggests a theory that equalizes advantage across the board. Chris Armstrong, *Justice and Natural Resources: An Egalitarian Theory* (Oxford: Oxford University Press, 2017). For a discussion of the arguments to which Armstrong is responding, see Michael Otsuka, *Libertarianism without Inequality* (Oxford: Oxford University Press, 2003); Peter Vallentyne, 'Left-Libertarianism', in David Estlund, ed., *Oxford Handbook of Political Philosophy* (Oxford: Oxford University Press, 2012), pp. 152–68.

7 Armstrong, *Justice and Natural Resources*, p. 247.

8 Other typical candidates are capabilities and resources.

9 Armstrong, *Justice and Natural Resources*.

10 The language of 'basic rights' might seem to suggest a very basic level of subsistence, but I do not make this inference. Subsistence can and should be defined

115

differently in different societies: since the idea is to identify the basic conditions for a flourishing human life, we would expect the level to vary depending on what is necessary to live a flourishing life in that society.

11 I insert the solar power condition to rule out the possibility of harmful by-products from consumption, which would change the analysis.

Chapter 3

1 Chris Armstrong, *Justice and Natural Resources*, chs 5 and 6, where attachment matters only if it supervenes on equality considerations; see also Lea Ypi 'Structural Injustice and the Place of Attachment', *Journal of Practical Ethics*, 5/1 (2017), 1–21.

2 Rawls and Buchanan use the term to describe an expectation that arises from institutions that are justified on grounds of justice, and argued that 'when these [rules] are just they establish a basis for legitimate expectations'. John Rawls, *A Theory of Justice* (Oxford: Oxford University Press, 1972), p. 235; Allen Buchanan, 'Distributive Justice and Legitimate Expectations', *Philosophical Studies*, 28/6 (1975), 419–25; for a discussion, see Alexander Brown, 'Rawls, Buchanan and the Legal Doctrine of Legitimate Expectations', *Social Theory and Practice*, 38/4 (2012), 617–44.

3 Alexander Brown, 'A Theory of Legitimate Expectations', *Journal of Political Philosophy*, 25/4 (2017), 435–60; Margaret Moore, 'Legitimate

Expectations and Land', *Moral Philosophy & Politics*, 4/2 (2017), 229–55.

4 Suzanne Goldenberg, 'A Texan Tragedy: Ample Oil, No Water', *The Guardian*, 11 August 2013; Suzanne Goldenberg, 'Fracking is Depleting Water Supplies in America's Driest Areas, Report States', *The Guardian*, 5 February 2014.

5 Kate Galbraith, 'West Texas Oil Field Town Runs out of Water', *The Texas Tribune*, 6 June 2013.

6 See Fergus Green, *Should Governments Provide Compensation for the Adverse Effects of Climate Regulation?* MSc in Philosophy at the London School of Economics, 2013. See also Lukas H. Mer and Pranay Sanklecha, 'How Legitimate Expectations Matter in Climate Justice', *Philosophy, Politics, Economics*, 13/4 (2014), 369–93.

7 'The Future of Electric Cars', *Open Access Government*, 1 November 2018.

8 Ypi, 'Structural Injustice and the Place of Attachment'.

9 Margaret Moore, *A Political Theory of Territory* (New York: Oxford University Press, 2015), ch. 3.

10 This argument has been used by Finland as part of a claim for their national parks being designated as a world heritage site. For the religious aspect of national parks, see http://whc.unesco.org/archive/websites/arctic2008/_res/site/File/Workshop_papers_and_presentations/07_presentation_Finland%20Saami_Norokorpi.pdf

11 See here both Daphne Barak-Erez, 'The Doctrine of Legitimate Expectations and the Distinction between Reliance and Expectation Interests', *European*

Public Law, 11/4 (2015), 583–601; and P. Sales and K. Steyn, 'Legitimate Expectations in English Public Law: An Analysis', *Public Law* (2004), 564–93.

Chapter 4

1 Miller, *National Responsibility and Global Justice*.
2 Jeremy Waldron, 'Rights in Conflict', *Ethics*, 99 (1989), 503–19, especially 515–18.
3 This is, of course, the central idea of John Rawls's *A Theory of Justice* (Cambridge, MA: Harvard University Press, 1971) and Murphy and Nagel, *The Myth of Ownership*.
4 Of course, a particular area may be of interest to more than one community. Think here of a river that is shared between two or more countries, in which case, institutional structures should be more complex, perhaps including shared forms of power-sharing, to realize self-determination. See here Cara Nine, 'When Affected Interests Demand Joint Self-determination: Learning from Rivers', *International Theory*, 6 (2014), 157–74; and David Miller, 'Debatable Lands', *International Theory*, 6 (2014), 104–21.
5 For useful suggestions about how to reform the international order in ways that would enable us to meet people's basic rights, see Thomas Pogge, *Global Poverty and Human Rights: Cosmopolitan Perspectives and Reforms* (Cambridge: Polity, 2012).

Chapter 5

1 Brian Barry, 'Sustainability and Intergenerational Justice', in Andrew Dobson, ed., *Fairness and Futurity: Essays on Environmental Sustainability and Social Justice* (Oxford: Oxford University Press, 1999), pp. 93–117.

2 Barry, 'Sustainability and Intergenerational Justice', p. 102.

3 *Ibid.*

4 Cecile Fabre, *Justice in a Changing World* (Cambridge: Polity, 2007).

5 See also Eric Neumayer, 'A Missed Opportunity: The Stern Review on Climate Change Fails to Tackle the Issue of Non-Substitutable Loss of Natural Capital', *Global Environmental Change*, 17/3–4 (2007), 297–301.

6 Cara Nine, *Global Justice and Territory* (Oxford: Oxford University Press, 2012). Nine does not defend this view, but she offers a very clear presentation of it.

7 For a good discussion of the specialized Arctic ecosystem and the disastrous effects of warming on it, see '$500bn Plan to Refreeze the Arctic' (*The Guardian Weekly*, 3 March 2017: 32).

8 United Nations Environment Programme, 'Rio Declaration on Environment and Development' (1992), available at http://www.unesco.org/educa tion/pdf/RIO_E.PDF

9 The dead zones in the oceans and many other water bodies are also connected to pollution from human

activities, such as fertilizer run-off, which leads to the spread of algae which dies and increases the calcification of the oceans. See www.scientificamerican.com/article/oceanic-dead-zones-spread/. Global warming also plays a significant role: www.smithsonianmag.com/science-nature/ocean-dead-zones-are-getting-worse-globally-due-climate-change-180953282/

10 Plastics pollution, coral bleaching, death of mangrove forests, etc., all at: https://www.marineconservation.org.au/pages/climate-change.html

11 For a terrifying analysis of the levels of carbon that would be released if the Arctic permafrost melts, read '$500bn Plan to Refreeze the Arctic'.

12 As Andreas Teuber has argued, 'If, as we seem to believe, it is wrong to cause another person harm without that person's consent, is it wrong to impose a risk of harm without consent?' A. Teuber, 'Justifying Risk', *Daedalus*, 119/4 (1990), 235–54 at 236.

13 Clearly this question cannot be answered only consequentially. We think there's something wrong with someone building a track that has a 50 per cent chance of collapsing, even if the train goes over it and the track doesn't collapse. See here Madeleine Hayenhjelm and Jonathan Wolff, 'The Moral Problem of Risk Impositions: A Survey of the Literature', *European Journal of Philosophy*, 20 (2011), 26–51.

14 Sven Ove Hansson, *The Ethics of Risk: Ethical Analysis in an Uncertain World* (London: Palgrave Macmillan, 2013), p. 102, original emphasis. See also John Oberdiek, *Imposing Risk: A Normative*

Framework (Oxford: Oxford University Press, 2017); and, in just war theory, there has been a great deal of discussion of risk as it is central to McMahan's account of liability in just war. See also Jeff McMahan, *Killing in War* (Oxford: Oxford University Press, 2009), and Seth Lazar, 'Limited Aggregation and Risk', *Philosophy & Public Affairs* (forthcoming).

15 Daniel Butt, 'Historical Emissions: Does Ignorance Matter?', in Lukas Meyer and Pranay Sanklecha, eds, *Climate Justice and Historical Emissions* (Cambridge: Cambridge University Press, 2017), pp. 61–79.

16 David Hume, *A Treatise on Human Nature*, ed., L. A. Selby-Bigge and P. Nidditch (Oxford: Clarendon Press, 1978 [1739]), pp. 484–98.

17 There are a number of transnational organizations that deal with areas of international cooperation over the Arctic and involve indigenous people. They are discussed in my paper, 'Is Canada Entitled to the Arctic?' Indigenous groups are important stakeholders in making decisions about the environment where they live or close to where they live.

18 For a discussion of different cost-sharing principles, see Armstrong, *Justice and Natural Resources*. For a similar argument to mine, applied to rainforests, see Chris Armstrong, 'Fairness, Free-riding, and Rainforest Protection', *Political Theory*, 44 (2016), 206–30.

Chapter 6

1 Moore, *A Political Theory of Territory*, especially ch. 3.